GETTING IN
THE WAY

Bertha Beachy

GETTING IN
THE WAY

Stories from
Christian Peacemaker Teams

Edited by Tricia Gates Brown

**Herald
Press**

Scottdale, Pennsylvania
Waterloo, Ontario

Library of Congress Cataloging-in-Publication Data
Getting in the way : stories from Christian peacemaker teams /
edited by Tricia Gates Brown.
    p. cm.
  ISBN 0-8361-9248-6 (pbk. : alk. paper)
  1. Christian Peace Maker Teams. 2. Peace—Religious
aspects—Mennonites. 3. War—Religious aspects—Mennonites.
I. Brown, Tricia Gates.
  BX8128.P4G48 2005
  261.8'73—dc22

                                        2005001923

Except as otherwise noted, Scripture is from the *New Revised Standard Version Bible,* copyright 1989, by the Division of Christian Education of the National Council of the Churches of Christ in the USA, and used by permission.

All photos courtesy CPT except page 72 by AP/Wide World Photos.

Is not this the fast that I choose:
to loose the bonds of injustice,
to undo the thongs of the yoke,
to let the oppressed go free,
and to break every yoke?

... If you remove the yoke from among you,
the pointing of the finger,
the speaking of evil,
if you offer your food to the hungry
and satisfy the needs of the afflicted,

then your light shall rise
in the darkness
and your gloom be like the noonday.
The Lord will guide you continually,
and satisfy your needs in parched places,

and make your bones strong;
and you shall be like a watered garden,
like a spring of water,
whose waters never fail.
Your ancient ruins shall be rebuilt;

you shall raise up the foundations
of many generations;
and you shall be called
the repairer of the breach,
the restorer of streets to live in.

Isaiah 58:6, 9-12 (NRSV)

Contents

Mexico

Colombia

Foreword

Christian Peacemaker Teams (CPT) was born in the 1980s during the chilliest times of the Cold War and the hottest of wars in Central and South America. We know that lasting peace and security can never come about through violence. No war will ever end all wars. All who take the sword will perish by the sword. Yet humans have spent thousands of years developing ever more lethal weapons. CPT offers an alternative to the sword: We have joined with the growing nonviolent peoples' movements of the past two decades who, in the words of Mary, have "scattered the proud" and "brought down the powerful from their thrones."

We know that disciplined, nonviolent peacemaking works. Already, in these few years, we have felt the power of Jesus's way to peace. We believe the presence of CPT helped limit the bombing of the critical civilian infra-structure in Iraq; prevented violence and deaths in particular confrontations in North America, Palestine, and Colombia; and reduced the risk of Chiapas, Mexico, sliding into a bloody civil war. All this was achieved by a handful of faithful volunteers and prayerful supporters. What might the Lamb's army yet achieve, with thousands, or tens of thousands, ready to walk onto the remaining battlefields of the world, armed only with the Gospel of Jesus Christ, and him crucified?

This work has not been easy. The stories in this volume honestly relate the deep questions that CPTers have as we confront our own racism and participation in the structures of violence and oppression. As Matthew Bailey-Dick writes, "Our first act of peacemaking must be to listen." The stories also relate the pain of those we accompany and the violence we have witnessed. Diane Roe writes that, "The human face that we helped

9

the world to see is still streaked with tears." The trauma of these encounters, and our own fears, doubts, and regrets, are shared here in powerful and moving accounts, along with our joys and hopes. Reflecting on her own fear and depression in Colombia, Carol Foltz Spring writes, "I am finding that embracing my fears somehow liberates me from them. Jesus's words to his fearful disciples, 'Why are you afraid? Have you still no faith?' remain a deep challenge as I struggle to be faithful to God. But I know I do not struggle alone."

One of the most inspiring aspects of these stories, and of CPT's work, has been the persistence and creativity of our peacemaking partners in each of these conflict zones. Their vision for a peaceful future, and their willingness to take risky steps to cross the divides in their communities, are a continuous encouragement to us as we walk with them along this path. As Matt Schaaf reports from Anishinaabe territory in central Canada, "The blockade has become a place for healing. Each visitor is afforded kindness and respect." Our partners in peacemaking have the bigger picture, and the longer perspective. They have taken the lead. As Anishinaabe teacher Charles Wagamese told us, "We have a responsibility to defend the Treaty, the land, and the children! Everyone's children! We are standing up for everyone!"

This work has only just begun. We can point to some successes, some failures, and much learning as we seek to overcome evil with good. We invite you, through these stories, to enter into this work, and then to join us in Getting in The Way. Joanne Kaufman concludes her story from Haiti saying, "We can never know or absorb the full impact of the stories we have told. We do hope, though, that our actions and our solidarity bear fruit far beyond our witness."

Doug Pritchard
Co-Director, Christian Peacemaker Teams
Toronto, Ontario, Canada
February 2005

Christian Peacemaker Teams:
An Introduction

Tricia Gates Brown

Before I began work with Christian Peacemaker Teams (CPT) in the summer of 2001, I thought of CPT the way I think of Amnesty International or the local Humane Society. It was an organization doing important, admirable work around the world, and I wanted to support it. Still, it was big, idealized, out of reach. Now that I have been working with CPT for a few years, it has taken on decidedly human dimensions for me. It has eyes, arms, and freckles. It gets giddy and uses colorful language. It sometimes says things it would like to take back. CPT is no longer an abstraction in my mind, but a group of specific people I've had the pleasure of meeting along my own CPT path. They are people who choose to live in conflict zones to create space for local efforts of nonviolent resistance. They talk to soldiers, guerrillas, and paramilitaries; they accompany school children and farmers; they advocate for human rights, support local initiatives in nonviolence, and disseminate reports of what they witness. But that is only part of the story—the glorious part.

The majority of their time is taken up with the daily grind of living in sometimes Spartan conditions: negotiating car repairs, figuring out who will do the dishes, holding lengthy team meetings based on consensus decision making, and spending countless hours visiting with local partners.

Christian Peacemaker Teams is simply a group of ordinary people doing ordinary things in extraordinary places. Occasionally, a small miracle happens, and they also do things beyond extraordinary.

When I think of CPT, I think of people like Stewart, a quiet and articulate man who exudes a deep pensiveness and tenderness, spawned in part from his days in Peace Brigades accompanying Salvadoran refugees out of their blood-soaked, fear-burdened land. I see him bantering with a Mayan boy in a dusty camp in Chiapas, Mexico, where he and I spent a few days among indigenous families displaced by paramilitary violence. I see him engaging in conversation with a military general outside one of the dozens of army bases scarring the Chiapas highlands. Stewart exemplifies civility, substantiating his opponents' humanity even while challenging and disagreeing with them.

When I think of CPT, I think of Char and Jessica. I see them laughing and chatting with police officers after being arrested for a symbolic action challenging the United States' second-largest defense contractor, while employees of the corporation stood by insulting them. Char, a gray-haired mother of three grown children, and Jessica, a former elementary school teacher, are pictures of gentleness and fun. Their mouths speak kind words, and their hands reach out to heal brokenness and halt abuse in their neighborhoods and in tattered corners of our world. The unassuming laughter of these women is like an eiderdown quilt.

CPT is people like Stewart, Jessica, and Char—ordinary people with big hearts and a passion for justice achieved nonviolently.

In this book, some of these people tell their personal, intimate stories of peacemaking work—of the moments of on-the-edge action and of the quiet moments when peacemaking is a shared cup of tea. This collection introduces readers to the work of CPT through the eyes and voices of those who *are* CPT. The honesty of these stories and the unpretentiousness of those telling them makes the singularity of the events all the more inspiring.

Christian Peacemaker Teams began in the fall of 1988, when Gene Stoltzfus, director of CPT from 1988 to 2004, became its first staff person. The organization was inspired by a speech delivered at an international gathering of the Mennonite Church, a speech in which Ron Sider, founder of Evangelicals for Social Action, challenged Mennonites to be "ready to start to die by the thousands in dramatic and vigorous new exploits for peace and justice." Anything less, said Sider, would be an admission that this group of committed, Christian pacifists "never really meant that the cross was an alternative to the sword." Sider's speech inspired the Mennonite Central Committee Peace Section and some representatives of the Church of the Brethren Office of Peace and Justice to dialogue about ways in which the historic peace churches could take bold new steps in peacemaking. Out of this dialogue, Christian Peacemaker Teams emerged. Others from the Religious Society of Friends (Quakers) soon joined the Mennonites and Brethren in sponsoring the project.

By 1992, several individuals had participated in CPT delegations to Haiti, Iraq, and the West Bank. These delegations helped the CPT Steering Committee to refine its vision for the organization and to recognize the need for a trained, full-time corps of peacemakers to carry out the work in conflict zones around the world. Full-time CPTers were recruited and trained. Their work was supported by reserve members, who committed to serving up to two months a year on CPT projects. Among CPT's first full-time projects were Haiti, Washington, D.C., and Hebron, in the West Bank. From the beginning, CPT has gone only to places where they've been invited and has always made efforts to consult local groups through patient, deliberate dialogue before acting.

The stated goal of Christian Peacemaker Teams is "violence reduction." CPTers stand in the way of violence by such acts as accompanying civilians threatened with violence. Teams also use conversation, video, photography, and journalism to discourage individuals in tense settings from acting violently. In addition, CPTers provide a "ministry of presence" by living in the thick of the conflict, choosing to reside in places of wearying tension. Sometimes this presence alone lessens the turbulence. It also allows CPT to respond more immediately and spontaneously as events unfold around them. At times, they literally "get in the way" and stand between aggressors and unarmed individuals.

In the countries where they work, CPT advocates for those

who have little voice in a conflict, often by talking to governments on behalf of individuals and by relaying stories from the field to communities and officials back home.

Finally, Christian Peacemaker Teams seeks to impact the Christian church by raising Jesus's call to peacemaking to a level of greater consciousness within the church and by enlisting the church in conscientious objection to war.

"Getting in the Way," CPT's motto, conveys multiple meanings. It denotes the practice of stepping between aggressors and victims, the practice of challenging structural violence and domination, and the practice of active nonviolence as taught by Jesus.

CPT offers a viable alternative to war. It has demonstrated that small teams of ordinary people trained in the skills of nonviolent intervention can make a striking difference in explosive contexts. People willing to stand in front of guns and lovingly challenge violence and domination truly diffuse tensions and protect lives in the midst of chaos.

At a time in human history when the incinerator of war is devouring countless lives and more resources than ever, people need to hear the stories of Christian Peacemaker Teams. This book offers vivid accounts of how regular people are reducing violence and working for peace. They are stories filled with hope for a better way. It is my hope that as you read them, you will be inspired to envision that better way and to see yourself as part of it. We can *all* be peacemakers.

CPT Fast Facts

At the time of this publication:

- CPT includes forty-five full-time corps members and 135 reserve corps members.
- CPT has full-time teams working in At-Tuwani and Hebron, West Bank; Colombia; Kenora, Ontario; and Iraq.
- Members of CPT have carried out full-time violence reduction work in Haiti; Bosnia; Chiapas, Mexico; Hebron; Washington, D.C.; Iraq; several indigenous communities in North America; and Colombia.

- CPT has hosted numerous delegations to these projects, as well as delegations to Chechnya, Afghanistan, and Vieques, Puerto Rico.
- Sponsoring bodies of CPT include Mennonite Church USA and Mennonite Church Canada, the Church of the Brethren, Friends United Meeting, the Baptist Peace Fellowship, and the Presbyterian Peace Fellowship.
- CPT is a grassroots effort supported in large measure by individuals and congregations. Full-time corps members are compensated according to need, and reserve corps members raise money to cover the cost of each of their trips.
- CPT holds two intensive, month-long trainings in nonviolence and peacemaking each year in Chicago, as well as occasional regional trainings in other parts of North America.
- Full-time CPT support staff are based in offices in Chicago and Toronto.
- For more information on CPT, see www.cpt.org.

Someone to Take Care of You

Jim Loney

December 16, 2002, The Farm, Durham, Ontario—Interview

The reporter begins with a predictable question: "Why do you want to go to Iraq?"

Putting my CPT training to good use, I have a sound-bite ready: "Just as soldiers are asked to sacrifice their lives for the state, as a Christian who believes in nonviolence, I believe that I must be prepared to make the same sacrifice."

"We are living in dark moral times," I add. "A time of lies and war, and lies to justify war." As the reporter scribbles, I think, "That sounded good."

Settling back in his chair, George Weber looks at me and asks, "What are you going to do if they start dropping bombs on Baghdad?" There is a twinkle in his eye, that devil's-advocate grin spread across his face. George and I trained together for CPT. Not one for prefabricated answers, he is testing me. Have I really thought through my decision?

I feel myself stumbling. I avoid the question. "War doesn't seem all that imminent. One thing that might happen is that the Iraqi government could evacuate us, just like they did with the Gulf Peace Team in 1991." I am conscious of an overwhelming desire to come home alive.

George, the seventy-three-year-old veteran world traveler, chuckles. "When the war comes, there won't be any government left to do anything. It will be chaos. What you'll need is two thousand American dollars in your pocket to hire someone to drive you out of the country. But don't worry." He smiles. "I'll look after you."

The interview continues. We explain that our twelve-day CPT delegation is going to join the Iraq Peace Team (IPT), a group of about thirty internationals associated with the Chicago-based organization Voices in the Wilderness. In the event of war, IPT will remain in Baghdad and take up stations at crucial civilian facilities, such as hospitals and water treatment plants, as a sign of solidarity. The hope is that our international passports will make American generals think twice about bombing those sites. We'll visit hospitals, schools, mosques, and churches, and meet with as many ordinary Iraqis as we can to learn for ourselves about life in Iraq.

"But what can you actually accomplish by going there?" the reporter asks.

George fields this question. "We are going to suffer with the Iraqis. It is an opportunity to light a candle rather than to curse the darkness."

When the interview is over and George is out of earshot, putting on his boots in the mudroom, the reporter, a local man I know, gives me a friendly punch on the shoulder. "You take care of George now," he says.

December 23, 2002, Sault Ste. Marie, Ontario—Doubts

I am walking through the grounds of my elementary school. I haven't been here for a while. It is very cold. Snow crunches noisily under my feet, and each invisible breath is exposed in a momentary plume of condensation.

George's question reverberates in my mind. "What are you going to do if the bombs start falling?"

When I decided to join CPT, I generally accepted the idea of laying down my life for peace. But am I ready to do that *now*? What if I am asked to pay some terrible cost? Am I prepared to embrace whatever happens, regardless of what that may be? I force myself to admit it: I am afraid.

The next morning, I attend Mass with my father. He goes every day. The words of consecration are like a blow to the stomach. *This is my body, broken for you. Do this in memory of me.*

After Communion, kneeling next to my father, I cover my face and pray. "God, I'm going to do this, even though I'm unsure. You're going to have to help me."

December 26, 2002, Toronto International Airport—Departure

"Merry Christmas, George."

"Merry Christmas, Jim."

We give each other a hug, the kind you can feel right through a winter jacket. We are on our way, pilgrims embarking for the unknown.

"You travel light," I say, pointing to his carry-on suitcase and shoulder bag.

"I've learned. Except I'm carrying the CPT laptop and the damn thing weighs a ton." I lift the suitcase. It is heavy.

Sitting in the departure lounge, we trade stories about our Christmas celebrations. I ask George how his children feel about his decision to join the delegation.

"We told them about ten days before Christmas. It just came up in conversation. My daughter said, 'Dad, I hope you're not thinking about going to Iraq with CPT.' So we told them. They didn't take it as badly as we expected. What do your parents think?"

"They're not very enthusiastic about it. We didn't actually talk about it much."

There is a pause. George looks out the window. Jets ferry back and forth. "You know, I've lived a long life, and it's been a good life. Of course I want to come back, but if I don't, I'm okay with that."

There it is again: that overwhelming I-want-to-come-back-alive feeling.

George laughs. "When I think of some of the taxi trips I've taken in Hebron, the way some of the drivers drive, I always think I'm much more likely to die in a car accident than I am 'getting in the way.'"

The time comes for us to board. I reach for George's suitcase. "Let me help you, George."

"Give me that," he says.

December 29, 2002, Baghdad—Arrival

It is a relief to step off the bus onto solid ground. I check my watch: 8 P.M. It's been a long day: 5 A.M. rising; a relentless roller-coaster ride on a Jordanian highway; stupefying expanses of desert; a two-hour rigmarole at Jordan's border; a three-hour

visit with a super-sized portrait of Saddam Hussein in the gar-
ish House of Senior Government Officials lounge.

My arms reach above my head in an involuntary stretch as
my body attempts to release its cache of nervous energy. We are
here.

George is collecting his bags. I reach for the computer.
"George, let *me* carry that." It has become a game: George complains about having to carry the computer; I make extravagant
offers to help; he refuses. This time I get to it first. "What would
I do without you?" he says.

Our sixteen-member delegation tramps into the lobby. Cliff
Kindy, one of our delegation leaders, motions for our attention.
"Don't get too comfortable, folks. Our minders want us to stay
at a different hotel. It's just a few blocks away." There is an
abandoned communications facility next door that could be a
target. "Put your things back on the bus, but don't go away.
Amal, who lives next door, has cooked supper for us."

It is true: In the hotel sitting room are heaping plates of rice
and chicken, an array of salads, dozens of pastries with savory
fillings—so much work! We are astonished by this prodigious
hospitality.

A few of us visit Amal and her husband, Samir, to thank
them. Amal is an elementary school teacher. Before the Gulf
War, she made 450 U.S. dollars a month. "Now I only make five
dollars a month," she says. "It is because of the sanctions."

After seventeen years of teaching, she had decided to quit.
Samir, whose English is better, explains, "It was costing her
more to go to work than she was earning." Now she works late
into the night, painting while her three children sleep. She sells
the paintings wherever she can.

When our visit ends, Cathy Breen, an IPTer from New York,
tells me their story is typical. "They've lost everything—their
home, their life savings. They rent this house. You can see the
middle classes down at the market selling their books, clothes,
appliances, just to get through another month."

December 30, 2002, Baghdad—Meeting

There is a tired-looking daypack on Cliff's knee. He pulls out
two-inch wads of Iraqi dinars, each held together with an elastic

band. "Here," he says, "you're going to need some money."

"How much is that?" someone asks.

"About twelve American dollars." He holds up one of the purplish bills. "Before the Gulf War, this 250-dinar bill was worth 750 American dollars. Now it's worth about twelve cents."

Gasps fill the room. We can't believe it.

"Courtesy of the sanctions," Cliff says.

He peers into his little notebook. "Okay, next item: contingency plans. As everyone knows, we're in a volatile situation here. There are a number of possible scenarios. Things could continue as they have been, without war, but with escalating pressure. Or the United States could begin bombing. One of the things they're talking about using is an experimental microwave bomb. It's supposed to fry the electrical grid and every electrical circuit within its range—computers, watches, hospital equipment, everything. Buildings stay standing. Nobody knows what it would do to human beings."

He continues: "The government could decide at any time to remove us from the country. Or, at any time there could be a coup. This is probably the most dangerous scenario for us. We could be arrested, held hostage, the whole society thrown into the chaos of civil war."

My heart starts beating faster. *That* feeling again. I had been thinking about staying on after the delegation for another two weeks. Now I'm not so sure.

"It's something everyone needs to think about," adds Peggy Gish, the other delegation leader. "There's a group from IPT that's preparing a contingency plan—stockpiling water, food, seeing if we can get a generator."

For our next meeting, we decide to break into small groups for an extended check in. The topic will be fears.

January 1, 2003, Baghdad—Hospital

Dr. Ahmed, the assistant director of the Saddam Hussein Central Pediatric Teaching Hospital, greets us in the lobby. "I am very glad to have some Americans here to show the effects of the embargo."

He brings us to one of the wards and introduces us to three-year-old Omar, who is curled up against his mother's chest. His face is ashen, his head swollen to the size of a basketball. A white bandage covers the left side of his face. Bruises encircle his right eye.

"Omar has cancer of the kidney. It metastasized to his brain and his eye. Since he is one and a half years old he has been restricted to bed. He has not even been playing with his brothers or sisters. The doctors and his parents, we are just waiting to say good-bye to him.

"Cancer in children has increased between 500 and 600 percent since the Gulf War. It can only be the depleted uranium used by the Americans. Omar's father was in the war.

"We can do nothing. The Americans do not even let us have the drugs we need. They do not even let us have heart medicine, glycerin. Do they think we will open every pill to make a bomb?

"Come with me," he says abruptly.

He leads us into another room and brings us to a bed where there is no child, only a bunched-up blanket. Dr. Ahmed looks at us. "A six-month-old baby was brought in to us last night. She had diarrhea. This morning, she died of dehydration."

There is an old woman, a grandmother, sitting on the side of the bed. Dr. Ahmed turns to her and asks gently, "Can we show the visitors your baby?"

Without looking at us, without saying anything, the woman moves to the next bed. Dr. Ahmed pulls the blanket back. Little Azhar is lying on her side, her face frozen in the manner of her last breath. Her eyes, her mouth are open, and there is a white film around her lips. Her tiny fingers are curled into a fist.

"Every day five to six hundred children are dying, just like this. It is because of the sanctions. We can't maintain our water treatment plants."

There are two more hospitals to visit after this one. At the next hospital, I overhear George: "I'll wait for you guys by the car." Thinking of his grandchildren, he can't bear to do it again.

Rosary

When I get back to my hotel room, I collapse onto my bed and pull out my rosary. The first prayer is the Apostles' Creed. "I believe in God, the Father Almighty, Creator of heaven and earth . . ." As I go around the rosary, bead by bead, I think how audacious, how futile, to profess faith in God in the face of this suffering—this evil, needless, unnecessary, *caused* suffering.

Then I think, perhaps this is the only thing that I can do, hold onto this circle of beads and profess it: *I believe in God.* And because I believe, everything within me must cry out: No to death. Yes to life. Again and again, around and around.

I make my decision. I will talk to Peggy tomorrow and tell her I would like to stay on with the team for another two weeks, as I had planned.

January 2, 2003, Baghdad—Breakfast

Anne Albright is the matriarch of our group. She is seventy-seven.

"Do you remember the doctor's name at Saddam Central Hospital yesterday?" I ask her.

"Yes. It's in my notebook here. . . . Dr. Ahmed."

"Thanks. I better write that down." I search my pockets. "Can I borrow someone's pen?"

"Here," George says, "you can have this one. I got a bunch at the market yesterday."

"Thanks, George."

George chuckles. "Somebody has to look after you."

Anne turns to George. "So you went to the market yesterday?"

"Yeah," George says, "I got a necklace for my wife, Lena." He is visibly excited by his choice. He shows it to us, an exquisite silver thread with a delicately tooled silver bead that moves freely along the chain.

The next round of coffee arrives. George is eager for a refill, but the coffee pot is beyond his reach. I pour some coffee into his cup. "Thank you," he says.

It's my turn to say it. "Somebody has to look after you."

Water

Hassan is my favorite person in Iraq. He is ten years old and works as a shoeshine boy outside our hotel. Yesterday the seat of his jeans was ripped open. Today his pants are torn at the knee. When he smiles, you can see that his front teeth are chipped, the permanent consequence of a close encounter with a car just a few days before. He is one of the millions of children in Iraq who, instead of going to school, work in the streets to help their families survive. It's another manifestation of the sanctions.

Hassan was given a miraculous gift, a soccer ball, from a Notre Dame priest who is a member of IPT. Hassan waves me over. He points to the soccer ball. His eyes are sparkling with invitation. I get into position. Hassan kicks the ball. His feet are clumsy. I kick it back. We are joined by a taxi driver and two policemen. Hassan tolerates them for a while, then abruptly dispatches them. He wants to play with me.

Hassan is suddenly thirsty. In the sidewalk, coming out of the ground, is a plastic tube, a public supply of water. One of the policemen is filling a jug to wash his car. Hassan runs up to him and he holds the tube out for Hassan to drink from. Earlier in the day, our team met with Mr. Wadah, the foreign ministry official responsible for international delegations. The first thing he said was, "Please. You must not drink the water. It is not good for us. You must only drink bottled water."

The average Iraqi child has fourteen episodes of diarrhea each year.

January 3, 2003, Al Kurnah—Eden

Having left the Iraq Peace Team behind in Baghdad, we are on our way to Basra. We turn off the main highway and speed through a market area in a convoy of three gleaming white Suburbans. Women sit on blankets with trinkets to sell. Men wheel pushcarts stacked with fresh produce in pleasing geometric lines. Little boys peddle trays of hot tea in glass tumblers. Everywhere heads are turning. A man catches my eye, sticks his thumb in his mouth, and then thrusts it in my direction. His eyes blaze with hatred. I suddenly understand why rich people like tinted windows.

The market gives way to a worn-out, hard-bitten neighborhood packed tight with flat-top, concrete houses. Bullet holes in walls testify to battles fought during the Iran-Iraq War (1980-88). Our convoy stops in front of a modest, family-run hotel that has seen better days.

"Why are we stopping?" I ask.

Tom Finger, a biblical scholar from Iowa, can barely contain his excitement. "This is the biblical garden of Eden!" I look around. Nothing distinguishes this place from any other. There's not even a plaque.

We go through the hotel into an L-shaped patio. At the point of the L, the Tigris and Euphrates rivers converge, form the Shat-al-Arab, and flow into the Gulf. We look down onto the river from a ten-foot floodwall. There's no way down to dip your feet in the water.

Everything is grey: the sky, the water, the land. The flat monotony is broken only by the occasional palm tree along the riverbanks. It is the most remarkably unremarkable piece of real estate I have ever seen.

"It is very beautiful," Zayde says. As one of our "minders," he is an official representative of the Iraqi government, responsible for approving and helping to organize our itinerary. There is a wistful look in his eye.

"Yes," I say.

A swarm of boys has gathered around our vehicles. There is a boys' school across the street from the hotel. Without thinking, I give one of them a leaflet written in Arabic and English that explains why we are in Iraq.

Suddenly, there is a sea of grasping hands in front of me. All of the boys want one, and I only have a few. There is a man standing among the boys, a teacher. I hand him one. He begins to read the leaflet, and the boys become very quiet.

> There was a teacher who was asked by his disciples, "How can we determine the hour of dawn, when the night ends and the day begins."
>
> "Is it when from a distance you can distinguish between a dog and a sheep?"
>
> "No," said the teacher.
>
> "Is it when from a distance you can distinguish between a rabbit and a mouse?"
>
> "No," said the teacher.
>
> "Tell us," they said. "When is it?"
>
> "It is," said the teacher, "when you can look into the face of another human being and you have enough light to recognize them as your brother or sister. Up until then it is night, and the darkness is still with us."

The leaflet goes on to explain that we have come from many different countries and walks of life, that we have come in peace to be brothers and sisters to the Iraqi people, that we don't want the sanctions, that we don't want war, and that we will stay in Iraq to experience what the Iraqi people experience, even if war does happen.

It is time to leave the garden of Eden. We get into our vehicles. The boy to whom I gave the first leaflet comes to the window where I am sitting. He waves shyly and says, "Thank you." We start moving, slowly at first, as we wait for the last vehicle to get organized. The boy trots beside us, waves, says, "Thank you." And then, as we drive away, the boy runs after us, waving, shouting, "Thank you! Thank you!"

The next day we learn that two days before, in the garden of Eden—the place where God gave us life, God gave us creation—Americans had dropped a bomb that killed one person and injured three others.

January 5, 2003, Basra—Night

I am sitting in the lobby of the Shaheen Hotel, staring out the window. It is 10:30 P.M. Bahar waves to me from the street, points to his shoes, then points to me. *Do you want your shoes shined?* I shake my head. *No.* I point to my watch, rest my head on my hands as if they are a pillow, then point to him. *You should be in bed.* He laughs and moves along, his portable workstation swinging at his waist from a shoulder strap.

The air-raid sirens begin their piercing wails. Coalition aircraft are in the vicinity, the sixth time today. No one bats an eye. We are suddenly plunged into darkness. The power is out for the third time today. The street fills with a ghostly wave of light as a car passes.

It has been a frustrating day. Our initial plan was to visit Safwan, a town near the Kuwait border that is polluted with depleted uranium. Zayde has been there one too many times. "Do you know," he says, "there was an Italian journalist who bent down to the ground to pick up something. Then he scratched his face. He got cancer in his cheek which spread to his bones." We would have to wear disposable overalls, masks so as not to breathe in any dust. Our Iraqi drivers would be at risk. We decided not to go.

"How many people live there?" I asked.

"Fifteen hundred families," Zayde answered.

So we spent the day being trucked around to a fishing port within sight of the Arabian Gulf; a mosque; a supper picnic on Sinbad Island, legendary home of Sinbad. Our minders wanted us to see the sights, enjoy ourselves. I wanted to learn more about the effects of the sanctions, meet people who could tell us about their experiences during the Gulf War.

"Could you take us to a place that the Americans have bombed recently?" I asked. "We would like to take some pictures to show people back home what is happening here."

"Yes, sure, no problem, anything you like," Zayde said. I couldn't understand it, but he was brushing me off.

The three minders accompanying us have been on perpetual edge. I assume it is because we are in the heart of Shia territory, an area that's fiercely opposed to the Sunni regime in Baghdad. They insisted on driving us to our meeting with Bishop Kassab, all of two blocks away. We are forbidden from taking walks or going to the market alone. Meetings with our Basra contacts have been awkward, strained. Their official presence has been stifling.

Tomorrow we return to Baghdad. I am looking forward to it. Our minders, at home in their element, will be much less solicitous and much less present.

The lights come back on. The shoeshine boy passes by the hotel again. He stops, repeats my go-to-sleep gesture, and waves goodnight. He is smiling. My sullen mood dissipates.

January 6, 2003, Basra—Accident

George gets into the Suburban first. Michele Naar climbs in next and sits beside George. She is surprised.

"George, what are you doing here? You never sit in the back seat. You always sit in the front, in the seat of honor. That's your place."

George laughs. "What, are you kidding? That's the death seat."

I sit in the middle of the middle seat. Charlie Jackson is on my left, Larry Kehler on my right. Pat Basler sits in the passenger seat. Except for Pat, none of us is wearing a seatbelt. Nobody wears seatbelts in Iraq.

At 7 A.M. our convoy pulls away from the curb, right on schedule. After a lunch stop at Ur, the ancestral home of Abraham, we will be in Baghdad by mid-afternoon. It is a glorious January morning, the sky infinitely blue and the desert bathed in lemon sunlight. There's not a car on the road.

There is an explosion of sound, thudding. I become acutely aware of the vehicle's orientation to the horizon. This is not good. Someone shouts, "We've lost a tire!" The vehicle starts to fishtail. I lean forward, brace myself against the front seats. Razza, our driver, is losing control. We skid to the right. No, he has it. We'll fall off the shoulder and ride it out. The back wheel catches against a curb. Our Suburban flips into the air.

The light goes grey. There is banging, crashing, sand flying. I am bounced up and down like a rag doll in a dryer. Conscious of every millisecond, I relax my body, tell myself not to fight, let it happen. I am accompanied by inexplicable feelings: everything's going to be okay; we're all going to make it; God saying, "I am with you, I am with you."

The bouncing stops. I am sitting on my head. My knees are touching my nose. My sense of up and down is all confused. I conduct a quick mental scan of my body: everything's there; I can move and feel everything. No pain. I'm all right. I push myself onto my knees. "Is everyone okay?"

I hear movement. "Yes," says a voice on my right. "I think so," comes from the left. I look around, there is light, and my eyes are open, but I can't see anything.

"Does anyone need help?" I ask.

"I'm okay," says one voice. "I can get out," says another. I'm not sure who is saying what.

The first thing I actually see is Michele jammed upside down in the back seat. Her head is pinned against her chest. Blood is flowing from the bridge of her nose.

"Michele, are you okay?"

"Yes, I think so," she says. "I can't move."

Oh, no. She's broken her neck. "Can you move your feet?"

"Yes," she says.

"I'm going to help you." I wiggle past, inches from her head, bend, and lift myself through the jagged edges of a smashed window. I'm out of the car. I can stand up. In the corner of my eye, I see Razza wailing uncontrollably, clutching his head with his hands.

Saffir, one of the other drivers, is suddenly beside me. He is frantic. He falls to his knees, grabs Michele by the shoulders, and starts to yank on her. I pull his hands back.

"We have to do this very carefully."

We lie on the sand, reach into the car, and gently deliver Michele from the wreck.

Shaking, Michele stands up and puts her hands to her temples. "I'm okay. I'm okay," she says.

I turn. Larry and Cliff are attending to Charlie. He rolls to his side, tries to get up, groans, "My back! My back!"

"Don't try to get up," we tell him. "Just rest." Somebody finds a jacket to put under his head. His face is white and contorted with pain. More people arrive. There seems to be plenty of help for Charlie.

"Is everyone out of the car?" I shout.

"Yes, I think so," somebody says. I walk toward the wreck but I can't bring myself to crawl back inside and check. I decide to circle the vehicle first to see if there is anyone lying hurt and unattended.

What's that? There's somebody on the sand. I can't tell who it is. I step closer. The face is an unrecognizable mass of blood, brain, and bone. "Who is it? It's Pat. I think it's Pat. Where's Pat?"

"I'm over here," Pat calls. He is attending to Charlie.

Those shoes, that shirt. "It's George. Oh, it's George." This can't be happening. LeAnne Clausen covers George with her jacket. I turn away. There's nothing that can be done.

"If there's any mercy in this," Anne Montgomery says, "he didn't suffer." Her face is ashen.

Charlie is being looked after. Everyone else is okay. By now, several dozen bystanders have gathered. There are odds and ends of luggage scattered everywhere. What are all these people *doing* here?

Razza! I can't imagine what he must be going through. I look for him. There he is, beside the car. Michele is sitting next to him, cradling him with her arm. He is literally choking on grief. I sit beside him, take his hand. He is blubbering inconsolably. "George, George . . . "

Zayde taps me on the shoulder. "We need your help with Charlie," he says. I follow him to where Charlie is lying. On signal, four of us pick him up and carry him to the back of one of our Suburbans, trying not to jolt his spine. Even with the back seat down, he barely fits. He has to lie with his knees bent.

"I want everyone who was in the accident to go in this vehicle. We will take you to the hospital," Zayde says, then points to me. "You stay with Charlie." I am relieved. Somebody has taken charge.

I crouch next to Charlie's head. There is no room for sitting. Anne is crammed beside Charlie's legs. "Are you going to be okay there?" we ask him. He nods, but he is not comfortable. We pack clothes around him so he won't roll, find something to put under his head.

It takes an eternity for us to get going. Zayde is rounding people up, giving instructions, supervising the transfer of our luggage to the other Suburban. Finally, we can leave. It is an excruciating ride back to Basra. I wrack my brain for small-talk ideas. We have to keep Charlie awake. Anne massages his hand; I stroke his head. His hair is full of sand, his face waxy. His

CPTer George Weber talks with soldiers while on a delegation to Chiapas, Mexico.

breathing becomes increasingly labored. "My chest. I can't breathe," he keeps saying.

The outskirts of Basra, finally! I can't believe what people are driving: wrecks on wheels held together with wire and duct tape. We pass a truck whose tires are worn right down to the cords. How ironic—our tires were brand new, our vehicle in mint condition. We pass a ragged band of children playing soccer with an empty water bottle. The lifeless earth of Basra rises in dust clouds about their feet. The world is still turning.

We stop at the hotel first. Zayde has to make phone calls. Charlie's breathing is reduced to a tortured hissing. He fights for each breath. "I . . . can't . . . breathe." His hands are cold, his lips turning blue. What is taking so long? Anne and I wave frantically to catch someone's attention. "Tell Zayde we have to go, now!" Another five minutes pass. I climb over Charlie to get out of the vehicle. "Zayde, we have to go to the hospital. Right now!" He waves, points, directs. The car fills again and we leave.

A doctor rushes out with a stretcher. All hands are on Charlie and he is lifted onto the stretcher. Saffir says, "Stay with Charlie. Don't leave him."

Charlie is wheeled into the emergency room. Curtains are flung back. An old woman sits on the next bed. She is gasping, clutching her chest. She can't breathe either. Her eyes are panicked, pleading for help. Her care has been usurped by the North Americans.

I collect Charlie's papers, watch, and wallet, and pass them to someone else. The doctor doesn't want to move Charlie, but his jacket needs to come off. He has a pair of scissors. The doctor looks at me, eyes questioning. I nod. He reluctantly cuts through the jacket.

"We need to get George," Saffir says. "Will you come with us?" I follow him out to an ambulance. I feel like I am in a dream. The conversation en route is fitful. We trade stories about the accident. Saffir asks about George's family. I ask about Saffir's family, his brother Razza.

Bob Leonetti, another member of the CPT delegation, greets us at the accident site. "Am I ever glad to see you guys!" he says. He looks like he's been through the wringer. Bob stayed behind to be with George and watch our luggage.

We are surrounded by men in uniform. Everyone seems to be talking at once, in Arabic. I have no idea what is going on. I am glad Saffir is standing beside me.

Someone who looks official asks in English, "You were in the car?"

"Yes," I say. His "clipboard" is a wafer-thin piece of cardboard.

"Your driver, he was good?"

"Yes."

"How fast was he driving?"

"One hundred and twenty kilometers per hour."

"It was an accident?"

"Yes." I am asked this sequence of questions over and over.

Saffir searches my face and says gently, "We have to move the body." I nod, but my head reels. Doesn't somebody else do this, a professional or something? In Canada . . .

We walk over to where George is lying. A stretcher is already there. Saffir and I stand on one side of George; Bob and the ambulance driver stand on the other. No one moves. It is a numinous moment.

Saffir elbows me. "Do you want to say a prayer?" It is more like an order than a request.

"Yes," I say. My mind reaches frantically. Something Bob and I can say together. "Our Father, who art in heaven, hallowed be thy name . . . "

The prayer is over. Now we can move.

"Did you check George's body?" Saffir says. "Make sure you have everything."

I look at Bob. It's been done. We reach down and lift George onto the stretcher. We carry the stretcher to the back of the ambulance, hoist it in.

I walk over to the wreck, bend down, and put several handfuls of sand into a plastic bag: some earth to bring back with George. Saffir comes up behind me and points to the bag. "Thanks be to God for you doing that," he says.

We are ready to go. I stop for one last look. I try to burn every detail into my memory: the exposed underbelly of the upside down Suburban; its angle in relation to the road; the long, arcing skid; the trail of glass in the sand; the curve of the road.

Rage

"Is there anything else?" the judge asks. He has been taking my statement.

"No. I think that's all."

"Thank you," he says.

I return to our team meeting, still in progress. The topic of discussion is our press release.

"I don't think we should wait any longer," someone is saying. "We've got to send it as soon as we can."

I interject. "Have all our families been contacted to tell them we're okay?"

By now the CPT directors back in North America, Doug Pritchard in Canada and Gene Stoltzfus in the United States, are aware of the accident.

"Doug and Gene are in the process of making the calls now. I think we can trust that it's being done."

"Yes," I say, "but how do we know if they've actually contacted our families. I don't know how other people are feeling, but I don't want my friend Dan finding out by e-mail that I've been in a car accident in which someone has died, or anyone else to find out that way, unless they explicitly say it's okay to go ahead. We need to check with everyone."

"Doug and Gene are making the calls. They'll eventually get through. We have to get this news out. We don't want our government to use this against the Iraqis."

"That's not good enough. I either want to talk to Dan myself or have confirmation that Doug has contacted Dan."

A group of us climb into one of the two remaining Suburbans. We're all wearing seatbelts this time. We're going to a phone exchange where we can make an international call. I am fit to be tied. I turn to LeAnne.

"I can't believe what happened at that meeting."

"I know," she says. "Everyone deals with trauma differently."

Oh, is that what it was?

The manager invites us into her office to make our calls. We give her the number and her assistant dials the number on a rotary phone. I suddenly realize that I haven't seen a single computer or cell phone since I arrived in Iraq. When it is my turn, I feel self-conscious. I don't want to make an emotional scene in front of all these people. The phone is ringing.

"Hello, Dan."

"James!" he explodes. "Are you all right?"

"I guess you've heard."

"Doug called me this morning at seven." That's 3 P.M. Iraq time. "I've been worried sick."

We don't talk for long. It's an awkward conversation. I want to tell him how much I love him, but I don't. This isn't a good place to say something like that.

After the call, I wait outside for the others to finish. There is a massive boom. I jump. The sky splits open in a roar of low-flying jets; the rising howl of air-raid sirens follows. Oh, the things I would do if I had a rocket launcher.

Back at the hotel, I feel lost. There's nothing *to do*. For the first time I become aware of a vast, aching, implacable empti-ness. I am unable to sit still. For just a moment, Zayde puts his arm on my shoulder.

"You are strong," he says. I am embarrassed and don't know what to say.

"This morning I had a dream," he continues. "We were trav-eling back to Basra. We had a car accident. In my dream it was the driver who was killed. That's why, when we got to the car, I was sure it was the driver. I was shocked when I saw that it was George."

Shivers ride up and down my spine. "Really?"

"Yes, it is true." The phone rings. Zayde has to go.

I run my hands through my hair. It's full of sand. There are bloodstains on my pants, bits of glass in my jacket pocket. "I should probably shower," I tell myself.

When we arrived three nights ago, the hotel had no towels. Zayde ran out to find some. There weren't enough to go around, so I used a shirt. Maybe now they have some clean tow-els. The thought is suddenly very exciting.

I go to the desk. "Yes," the clerk says, "we have clean tow-els." He waves two of the staff over. They take me into an office. There is a pile of towels heaped on a chair. They look sus-piciously familiar. One of the men picks up a towel and folds it carefully over his arm. "Follow us," he says. He takes me up to my room, opens the door and, with an officious flourish of hands, places the towel on its hook. "There you are, sir." I dig in my pocket for the obligatory tip.

The towel is wet, one of our few towels they collected after we left three days ago. I feel like throttling the staff.

And then it strikes me. I'm here. I'm alive! I'm alive to shiver through a cold shower and dry myself with a secondhand towel. I turn on the tap and brace myself for an onslaught of cold water, but to my delight the water is hot. I stand under the faucet, and I can feel *every single* drop of water, and every cell in my body sings with the joy of it: *I am alive!*

When I'm done, I wipe my beloved body dry. My beautiful, amazing, miraculous body. I wipe it all dry with my secondhand towel. Thanks be to God for secondhand towels. Thanks be to God for *everything.*

January 7, 2003, Baghdad—Greetings

"Jim! Jim!" Hassan runs up to me, grabs my hand. "You're back!"

I laugh. "Yes, I'm back. I'm so happy to see you."

"Shine shoes? Shine shoes?"

"Yes," I say. "They really need it." I rest my foot on his portable footstool. He sits on an old paint can. He works vigorously. When he is done, he points proudly to his little friend sitting next to him. "Jamal. Baby shoe shine. Baby shoe shine." His first day on the job.

Abdullah greets me at the door of the hotel. He is the door-person. "Jim! We heard about George. We can't believe it. I am sick. We are all so sad. Did George have any family?"

"Yes," I tell him. "His wife, Lena, two children, and four grandchildren."

"Oh, that is terrible. We like George so much. He is so nice. We think he is funny. We call him 'Mr. Canada.'" Abdullah points to his chest, recalling the Canadian flag lapel pin that George always wore. "For us, in our religion, George is a martyr. He died for something good."

January 9, 2003, Baghdad—Phone Call

A deep breath. "Hello, can I speak to Lena please?"

"This is Lena."

"Hi, Lena. It's Jim Loney." I was with George. I *was* with George.

"Jim! Where are you?"

"I'm calling from our hotel in Baghdad."

"Thank you for coming home with George. You don't know how much this means to us." Her voice is strong.

I'm embarrassed. "Well . . . it's something I want to do." *Somebody has to take care of you.*

"How are you?" she asks. "You've been through so much. It must've been . . . terrible."

"It . . . it was. I'm okay. I was really lucky. I escaped with just a sore knee. How are you doing? I can't imagine what you must be going through."

"I'm coping. Sometimes I just can't believe this is real. The hardest thing is the waiting. In a way, I'm kind of lucky because we were all together for my brother's funeral when the news came."

"I'm sorry I haven't called until now. I was waiting to have something firm to tell you. I've got a flight arranged for George and me tonight, from Baghdad to Amman. George is booked through to Toronto, but I'm not on the Amman to London flight. We'll just have to cross our fingers and hope for the best. If we're lucky, I should be home with George by midnight tomorrow, your time."

"Friday night, that soon! Doug told me it might take a week. I don't know what I would do if it took that long."

There is a pause. "Did you pick up George's suit?" Lena asks. George ordered a custom-made suit from a tailor next to the hotel before we left for Basra. He said it was his way of helping the local economy.

"Someone from the Iraq Peace Team picked it up. It's been taken to the hospital morgue and George's body is being prepared right now. If everything goes according to plan, the body will be released this afternoon."

"What's it been like for you, making all these arrangements?"

"It's been a little stressful." In some ways, more stressful than the accident itself. Not speaking any Arabic, not knowing how anything in this society works, I feel like I've been swinging from one trapeze to another, never knowing if I'm going to catch the next one.

"But, somehow," I tell her, "I don't know how, it all seems to be working out." It's that feeling again: *I am with you. I am with you.*

"Lena, I'm sorry to ask you this so soon. It's so early and you're still trying to make sense of everything. But Razza, our driver, is in jail. It's how they do things here. The driver is responsible and they're going to hold him until it's clear whether any claim is going to be made against him."

"Doug told me about that."

"Take the time you need to think about it. I don't want to put any pressure on you, but they need a letter from the family saying they understand it was an accident and they aren't making any financial claim."

"I'll write the letter. You say it was an accident. You were there. I trust you. I certainly don't want to keep an innocent man in jail."

I take a deep breath. Lena is incredible.

March 8, 2003, Durham, Ontario—Vigil

There are twenty of us standing at the one intersection in town that has a traffic light. It is one of those days people call "glorious": blue, fresh, clear, and if you stand in the sun, actually warm. Maple syrup season.

Our signs read, "No blood for oil," "An eye for an eye makes the whole world blind," "Honk for peace." It is our weekly Saturday vigil against the war. I am standing beside someone I haven't met before, a woman in her early forties. She is resting her arms on a stroller.

"Hi, my name is Jim." We shake hands.

"I'm Hazel. This is my grandson Kalvin." A little boy hides behind her leg.

"Are you the one who went to Iraq?" she asks.

"Yes," I say.

"You were with George?"

"I was. Do you know George?"

Her face lights up. "He was my history teacher in high school. That man had a profound effect on my life. I didn't realize it until years later though, when I thought about the things he would say. It was the kind of questions that he made me ask.

He always made you think. You couldn't take anything for granted with him."

"I know what you mean," I say.

In the accident that killed George Weber, Charlie Jackson suffered two cracked ribs and three fractured vertebrae. He remained in a Baghdad hospital until his return to the United States on January 19, 2003. The Iraqi government covered all of his medical expenses. Charlie was still recovering when he returned to Iraq on another CPT delegation in December 2003.

This Place Where My Feet Stand on the Earth

Matt Schaaf

December 3, 2002, Slant Lake

"I was born here! Right here at Slant Lake! This was a Mando camp and my Dad logged with a horse. All of us kids went to school in a little trailer." Jim Ambs, of Ambs Forest Products, argues before a crowd of about thirty Ojibway high-school students and women from the Grassy Narrows First Nation. The native protesters stand on the road in the path of a fully loaded pulp truck bound for the paper mill. Ambs' four-by-four pickup, door ajar, idles behind him.

"Time to move on! Go home!" someone shouts from the back of the crowd. Anger hangs in the cold air.

Ambs persists, "You guys have got the wrong end here. You've got the wrong end. You got to talk to the company. I just go where I'm told. What this is . . . this is just trouble!" he sputters.

"We've got the right end," retorts Joe Bill (JB) Fobister, a blockade spokesman. JB is a quiet man. He runs the local store. His voice is low, but he's angry, and shaking. Behind him stand a dozen silent women.

All around us, young, brilliant-green spruce trees line the bush road, the road where Ambs Senior must have skidded logs with his team of horses, the road where a few moments ago, a semi-truck loaded with jack-pine logs scrunched to a chilly halt on the snow. Its progress was blocked by a dozen students from the Grassy Narrows Indian Reserve high school. Standing in the middle of the road, the students wielded signs in bright colors:

"Respect Our Land" and "We Believe in Traditional Land, Not Clear-cutting."

An Ontario Provincial Police (OPP) officer, head shaven bare, trails a frosty plume from his lips when he speaks to the students. "You can't block a provincial road like this. Everyone has to go home." The young officer must be working hard to look so stoic in minus thirty Celsius (about minus four Fahrenheit).

"Hey, how fast does your truck go?" asks one female student, and soon the youth have the officer joking with them.

I step into the circle of protesters and police, and offer my hand to Ambs. "My name is Matt Schaaf and I'm with Christian Peacemaker Teams. The community here"—I wave my hand around the gathered knot of teenagers, school teachers, community women, and JB—"has invited us as peaceful observers. It's our job to make sure no one gets hurt here."

Ambs perfunctorily shakes my hand and goes back to pressing his case with JB. Two young community members capture the scene with their digital video cameras.

The high-school students have chosen to make their stand against clear-cut logging about five kilometers north of the Grassy Narrows Indian Reserve in Ontario. Trappers and community leaders have spent years slogging through the proper channels to protect their forest home from being razed by pulp and paper giant Abitibi-Consolidated. Yet the clear-cutting continues, and a handful of residents are taking action to stop the logging themselves. They've picked a cold winter day to do it.

In 1999 I visited this Ojibway community of about seven hundred residents as a short-term delegate with Christian Peacemaker Teams. About three hours from my home in Winnipeg, Manitoba, the road began to wind in a stomach-turning ride deep into the spruce, pine, and aspen of the boreal forest. Countless glacial lakes bordered the treacherous route. At the end of the road, I learned from Grassy Narrows' chief that their Nation signed a treaty with the Canadian government in 1873 to guarantee peaceful relations between newly arrived white settlers and the native communities dotting the numerous waterways of their ancestral territories.

I met with the Environment Committee, a half-dozen committed mothers, grandmothers, and teachers, and learned that three years after the treaty was signed, the Indian Act legislation had gathered people onto small reserves. The Ojibway watched hydroelectric dams flood their wild rice fields and burial grounds. The unearthed bodies of buried relatives floated through the waterways of the community. In 1963, the Canadian government pressured the Ojibway to leave their riverside homes and concentrated them onto a new fourteen-square-mile reserve. Neighbors and kin were split up. Access to alcohol increased as a road was built into the new site. And in 1971, 150 commercial fishing jobs were lost when the government announced that more than fifty metric tons of mercury had been dumped into the river by the pulp and paper mill Reed & Company.

To this day, many in the Grassy Narrows community, which is highly dependent on fish for its diet, suffer early blindness and nerve damage from heavy-metal poisoning. As late as 1975, Ojibway children were taken from their parents to government-funded residential schools run by church groups. Separated from their families, the students were punished for speaking their language and taught to be Christians.

The clump of young people now blockading trucks in the roadway won't be moved. A cheer goes up as the heavy pulp truck grinds into reverse and backs down the road. Ambs leaves off arguing, gets in his truck, and pulls away toward town, shaking his head in frustration. An OPP sergeant arrives from Kenora, the nearest white logging town, and converses quietly with JB, eye to eye in private conference. The sergeant motions for attention. "Under the Canadian Charter of Rights and Freedoms, you have the right to protest here. As long as this demonstration remains peaceful, the OPP will not get involved."

On the wind-scoured roadbed, deep in the boreal forest, the students raise their signs and cheer.

December 5, 2002, Grassy Narrows Traditional Land-Use Area

JB's red, mud-spattered four-wheel-drive truck bucks through the rutted remains of someone's trapline. I sit wedged between the bucket seats, and my head hits either the roof or the rearview mirror at each jolt. My teammates and I have packed ourselves into the cab so JB can show us what a clear-cut looks like. It looks like the moon.

Ruts, stumps, unused tree limbs and trunks, and a few standing dead aspen ("weed trees" in the parlance of the forest managers) foul several square miles of empty space that used to be thriving boreal forest. Smoldering heaps of slash (leftover branches and logs) send up thin smoke into the overcast sky. The slash piles tower above our heads.

JB describes growing up on the trapline with his parents: "All we needed was a tent, a rifle, tea, sugar, and salt, and to learn to hide in the bush the day the Indian agent came to take children away to residential schools." We learn that the Ojibway call themselves and their language Anishinaabe (Uh-nish-uh-nawbay), which means "the natural people." JB teaches me to say the name of the community in Anishinaabe: Asubpee-schoseewagong (Uh-sub-shko-seewah-gongk). It takes me ten or twelve tries to get my tongue around it. I feel like a slow learner.

"Asubpeeschoseewagong," JB explains softly, "means web-like grass." He takes his hands from the wheel for a second and interlaces his fingers like a net. He points out a path leading to his father's trapline. "The Anishinaabe have trapped, hunted, and fished here for as long as anyone can remember." He hauls the truck to the right, up a steep, rocky trail, and we're in another clear-cut, this one even larger than the last. We tumble out of the cramped cab to stretch our legs for a moment. All around us, stumps and sky, decimated earth. "I feel dizzy," murmurs JB to himself.

December 6, 2002, Jones Road

Teammate Scott Kerr and I leave Kenora after dark with a load of winter boots and groceries in the back seat of our Geo Prism hatchback. The team has grown to three people while the temperature has dropped again into the minus thirties Celsius. Scott and I laugh and recall stories from CPT training, which we attended together in Chicago, and from our work in Chiapas, Mexico. The last time I had seen him, we had been accompanying fishermen on the jungle rivers of Colombia.

By now we are accustomed to the ice-paved switchbacks between Kenora and the reserve. We're deep in conversation about the South American rainforest when we realize, too late, that the next snowy turn doubles back on itself. I have time to say, "Don't touch the brake!" then we're sliding sideways toward the frozen lake—to the right, then left, across the oncoming lane. A steel culvert is the next thing I see rushing toward us in the headlights. Then blackness.

Upside down in the air, I hear the soft thump of snow on the roof. Our little car eases underwater to the groan of fractured ice. In the pitch black, I guess that I'm hanging from my seatbelt with my knees on the ceiling, somehow still conscious. Scott is awake too.

"Are you okay?" he asks calmly.

Water pours in along the door seals. It must be cold, but I can't feel it. In a few seconds, our seatbelts are off. But where is the door lock? I'm right side up in an upside-down car, sightless in the dark. Suffocating seconds pass while my fingers scramble for the lock. There is water to my waist. Somewhere in the back of my mind a ludicrous voice reminds me: *You hate drowning, you always said you never wanted to die this way.*

The lock is in my fingers, then the door handle. I push out against the black pressure. The car door won't move more than an inch. Lake water pours into the cabin. I hear Scott searching faster and faster for his door handle.

I brace my knees against the inverted dash and place my hands on the crumpled, paralyzed door. I've got one more try. This time it shifts and creaks outward, scraping ice. Through the inrush of water, I scramble for the surface to find myself standing on a creek bottom in three feet of December water, wet only to the waist.

Scott is out right behind me, soaked to the neck. Still standing among the bobbing, icy shards, I reach into my pocket and start to laugh. My fingers have closed on a dry book of matches. Together we climb the slippery snowbank to search for dry firewood, but it proves unnecessary. Within five minutes a community member drives up, and we climb into the warm pickup, heading for the reserve.

Inside the truck, shaking, I tell our astounded rescuers how we escaped the flooding car. Frozen in my mind is a picture of Scott waist deep in the pool, the puzzle pieces of ice bumping his thighs, the headlights burning sightlessly under the ice in the utter silence of the dead engine.

January 20, 2003, A trailer on the Grassy Narrows Reserve

The Anishinaabe haven't always lived on fourteen square miles of infertile land. Roger Fobister, vice-principal of Sakatcheway Anishinaabe School in Grassy Narrows, spreads a map across the floor of our borrowed house trailer. Hundreds of lakes, each with an Anishinaabe name printed beside it, sprawl across 2,500 square miles of traditional territory.

"In the winter, families lived on traplines scattered along the waterways," explains Roger with his lyrical voice. "Whole families—ten to twelve people, including grandparents and children—wintered in a small cabin. After the ice broke up, they would gather here to fish."

He points to the Old Reserve. "In July, the blueberries would ripen and everyone would go to this area to pick them." Roger indicates several lakes southwest of the Old Reserve. It looks like a long walk.

"The wild-rice harvest would begin in August or September. Everyone camped around Stewart Lake and went out in canoes to gather the rice and process it right there. Then it's time to head back to the trapline before freeze-up."

Roger began the Anishinaabe language program at the school. With the help of community elders he had this map printed, showing the names of waterfalls, rivers, lakes, and bays in their own language, proving that the Ojibway had always been there. Also an entrepreneur, he pushes his people to become economically self-sufficient, recognizing that 75 percent of the reserve population is unemployed.

"I started a business for my son," he says. "We take contracts from Abitibi to plant trees, thin them in summer, and log in the winter months. I guess I keep about eight people off the welfare roll and save the government a lot of money."

"And the closing of logging roads to Abitibi's contractors by other Asubpeechoseewagong citizens?" we wonder.

"I guess I'm trying to remain neutral."

January 23, 2003, Slant Lake

At Slant Lake, CPTers accompany the protesters twenty-four hours a day through mid-winter. The sun appears after 8 A.M. and sets at four in the afternoon. Blockaders and CPTers escape the mind-numbing wind by huddling around a wood-burning stove in a trapper's cabin. A spiritual leader performed four days of ceremonies to light a sacred fire that will be kept burning until the blockade—now fifty days old—ends.

Though the men keep the sacred fire, it is the women of Asubpeechoseewagong who birthed the Slant Lake camp and who nurture its spiritual focus. Judy daSilva and her four children spend most of their time at the blockade. Her sister Roberta drives over after finishing work at the Band Office each day. "Our commitment to keeping the fire going represents our commitment to the land," Judy says.

Their brother, Robert Williamson, raises a canvas tipi on fresh spruce poles over the sacred fire to keep out the weather. Chrissy Swain brings a hand-drum and the women sing every night in the tipi while they wait for logging trucks to arrive. One woman is nine months pregnant. A draft carries the smoke up the tipi walls, past the wind flaps—the fire sparking against the starry sky.

A few mysterious pickups drive by in the early morning to see if blockaders are still active, then turn around for Kenora. The drivers clutch CB radios tight to their mouths. The women's voices and the steady drumbeats swell: "Great Spirit, help us. Great Spirit, help us." How long have they sung those words—while picking blueberries, or setting beaver traps, or tramping through the bush in search of dry firewood to keep the sacred flame alive?

I am slowly getting a feel for the lilt of Anishinaabe spoken around me during the long nights. "*Omaa kaa ti na kii yaan*—that's how we would say traditional land-use area," Robert tells me. "Oh-mah. Kah-tih-nuh-kee-ahn. It means 'this place where my feet stand on the earth,' or 'where humans roam.'" It takes me six tries to say it.

April/May 2003, Wilcox Lake Trapline

Don Billard and I pull our boat over a sandbar into a bay at the foot of a steep, wooded slope. We thrash our way through the willows and thistles, and tumble onto an open shelf of old yellow cedars. It must have once been a lake. A pure stand of red pines crowns the hill—some too big to wrap your arms around.

I've come to Andrew "Shoon" Keewatin's trapline for a week with Don, Shoon's assistant. Shoon estimates that 75 percent of his line (a total area of approximately 120 square miles) has been logged, and the red pines appear on this year's cutting schedule. Don will guide me as we document the Abitibi contractor's activities.

Our boat navigates the granite cliffs and broad-backed rocks of the English River channel, as Don points out that we are steering through the remains of the Ice Age. Over billions of years, the glaciers withdrew, scraping off the tops of these ancient mountains, leaving only the granite roots exposed. He reminds me that many generations of Anishinaabe walked every square foot of these mountain roots. Yet we see only a few stone arrowheads as evidence of their presence. Today's generation has been enclosed on the reserve.

Each long afternoon Don and I tramp through what is left of the bush, counting logs left behind by the contractors—381 in one afternoon—examining replanted trees, photographing oil containers and pop cans left by loggers and white moose hunters. Walking, walking, walking. Government bureaucrats, environmentalists, trappers, and loggers hold a deafening debate in my head: A clear-cut emulates a forest fire. . . . No, fires leave behind trees and ash. . . . (walking, walking) . . . The herbicides are proven to be safe. . . . Stop poisoning our Mother! . . . (walking) . . . Have you studied Forest Management?

I shut out the arguments. This much is clear: people who live in cities and towns decide how to manage the trees, while the people who live in the forest are ignored. It doesn't escape me that I am an outsider. I grew up in a logging town and have managerial tendencies all my own.

We pause to shoot a picture of an oil filter, to examine a wood frog, to pick up a moose antler. When we've hiked ten minutes beyond the spot where we picked up the antler, Don exclaims, "I forgot to leave tobacco! Wait here." The Anishinaabe habitually put loose tobacco on the ground when picking berries, cutting trees, or taking animals. It is a sign of thanksgiving, and reminds them that the animal or plant has given itself as a gift.

"I am getting to be like those guys at Abitibi!" Don fumes. "I think I can take something just because it's there."

June 10, 2003, Garden Lake, New Reserve

Shoon taught me the Anishinaabe word for white man: *wempitigozhe*, "men who take the trees." The first European explorers arrived on Lake of the Woods in 1644, and the loggers were hot on their heels.

We pour handfuls of wild rice in a depression in the ground and stamp on it to remove the husks.

"As native people we were taught to take only what we need and to leave the rest for others," Shoon explains. He thinks this conservationist attitude made it easy for his people to accept government welfare, because the hunters could then save the animals for harder times.

The rice we are processing was harvested from the tall, light-green rice grass growing in the shallows and shores of the river system. One person poles the canoe through the grass while a second harvester knocks the ripe grains into the bottom of the boat with two sticks. After curing the rice on a fire, people tie on clean moccasins and dance on the roasted grains to loosen the husks, which are then winnowed away. If stored in a dry place, the rice lasts for years. People feast on it. The first harvest is processed and cooked, and the entire community is invited to a celebratory meal, giving thanks that the crop is enough for the people.

There is a stab of sadness in me. I am of the people who leave rotting heaps of logs and know little about feasts or arrowheads.

January 30, 2003, Slant Lake Camp

"When the whites first came to our land, they brought the Bible. We shared everything we had with them. Now the whites have the land and the Indians have the Bible. Pretty bad deal!" Steve Fobister, deputy chief and a blockade spokesman, laughs ruefully. He perches across the fire from me, the plume of smoke erasing and redrawing his face.

When I was a theology student in Winnipeg, our Old Testament Bible professors lectured on the covenant the Hebrew people had with their god, Yahweh. It was a sacred agreement. The Scriptures use the same Hebrew word we translate as "covenant"—*berith* (bey reet')—to describe treaties and arrangements between nations.

One hundred and thirty years after signing Treaty #3, the sacred nature of this crucial agreement continues to elude Canadians. Our Christian tradition provides us the strength to live in a sacred, reciprocal relationship with First Nations, but instead we bring flooding, residential schools, deadly mercury, and clear-cut logging. We have the land. The Indians have only the Bible.

February 1, 2003, Journal Entry

Thinking of CPT's motto: Getting in the way. We need to get *out* of the way here. My people have been in the way too long. I came to Grassy to accompany a logging blockade and reduce the chances of people getting hurt, but the blockade has become a place for healing. Each visitor is afforded kindness and respect, no matter who his or her ancestors might be: Anishinaabe, German, Japanese.

The government's Royal Commission Report on Aboriginal Peoples proposes self-governance and healing between nations. Churches and NGOs [nongovernmental organizations] deliver position papers on reconciliation. Courts level their version of justice in residential school abuse cases. But it is the blockade that doctors us. All of us, huddled together against the minus forty windchill. Can it last?

February 6, 2003, Junction of Segise Road and Highway 671

9:40 A.M. We've been on this deserted logging road for almost two frigid hours and everyone is ready to go home. Since eight this morning, about twenty men from the reserve and a supporting cast of Okiijida warriors and CPTers (myself and

Murray Lumley from Hamilton), have stood at a roadside fire, waiting for the appearance of logging vehicles.

Steve Fobister draws a gray line of ash and ember across the road with his shovel. Carefully, he lays it down in the snow from one ditch to the other. "Ha! Let them try to cross this line," he cackles. He has angled his two-door Pontiac across the width of the washboard road.

No trucks.

A community member reported seeing a pulp hauler on this route to the mill in Kenora, though truckers have been warned not to use this road. The blockaders want them to take the long way—double the miles—through Vermilion Bay, so they've set up a temporary blockade. But we've seen nothing thus far. Finally, Steve heads for his car and we kick at the fire, grab our cameras, and start toward our own truck. Logging trails crisscross, web-like, through the forest, too numerous to blockade simultaneously. So community members take their chances— one blockade at a time.

There's a faint rumble from the east. Everyone freezes. Then, as the semi takes the curve, there is a growl of gears, a roar of downshifting.

We restart the fire and wait for the appearance of the truck. People nervously position themselves in the road. The truck grinds back and forth through the bush, up and down the seam of the road, scarred into the ground. Like an angry bear it signals its approach.

Headlights sweep around the final curve, and three Anishinaabe men stride toward the oncoming vehicle: a fully loaded Western Star tractor, bound headlong for the mill. It had gambled on the shortcut—and lost. The blockaders' hands are raised, palms toward the high windshield.

There is a tense moment between the instant the tractor and its jack-pine load slam shivering to a halt before Steve's ash line, and the first exchange of words. Community people huddle to select a spokesperson. Murray stands alone, with video camera locked on the semi's cab. Through the darkened windshield, the driver's eyes are steady on the people and cars blocking his path. A CB handset presses to his lips.

～ ～ ～

A member of the Asubpeeschoseewagong community stops a logging truck from passing during a blockade of a main logging road.

11:15 A.M. Robert Williamson acts as spokesperson for Grassy Narrows. He informs the first driver that he will have to turn around and go back the way he came. A police SUV pulls up and a couple of local officers spill out. Their sergeant from Kenora, Bob Reid, makes the trip from town to play a negotiating role.

I float down the queue of impotent machines. One truck pulls a machine with a mechanical grapple arm and a three-foot diameter circular saw, called a "slasher." It has drawn up behind the pulp truck, along with two four-wheel-drive pickups, bearing the operators. I greet each driver, introducing myself ("Hi, Dave, remember me from Deer Lake Road?"), explaining that human-rights observers are present to make sure no one gets hurt. Chatting. ("First run of the day, guys?")

Now the long and wearisome haggling begins. Bargains, offers, and cajoling are carried from semi trucks to fireside protesters by officers in parkas. Robert listens without speaking to the loggers or police. When they finally wind down, they look to him for a response.

"You'll have to go back the way you came."

The drivers scale the sides of their vehicles, clamber, disgusted, into high cabs, and wait for the next round of back-and-forth. Rob Ambs doesn't mind telling me how he feels.

"This is just hurting the little guys," he says. "This doesn't touch Abitibi! Our family is leaving because we've lost so much money this winter. You guys are really getting to *us*, but nothing's changing. We're leaving and not coming back for at least two years. Why don't they just let us get our equipment out and go home?"

(Four months later Rob's brother, Jim, will straddle his ATV and tell me through my car window that Abitibi-Consolidated sent them back to this area, that he had to take the contract or lose money. He has bills to pay. "These people at Grassy got to understand that this is the real world. The *real* world. I'd love to do selective cutting. I even proposed it to the company. But there's no money in it.")

4:00 P.M. Through the OPP officers, the blockaders agree to allow trucks to proceed about one hundred meters to the highway in order to turn around. The truckers agree to return the way they came. Car doors open and slam, keys turn in their ignitions, cameras pan with the trucks as they crawl toward the paved highway.

Dave turns his semi onto the asphalt first, but heads north toward the reserve and Slant Lake. This was not the agreement. Someone from Grassy pulls her four-wheeler grill-to-grill with the slasher so it can't follow. The remaining drivers offer that maybe their comrade is using another side road to turn his vehicle. The skeptical four-by owner does not withdraw.

Dave's truck revs around the bend, facing town, and he announces he can't possibly go back the way he came. There is a dangerous hill—too steep. He demands, "Who'll pay for the rig if I slide backward and bend the trailer?"

Protesters are now blocking a provincial highway—a much

more serious offense than blocking the bush road they had closed down in the morning. Robert and I observe the OPP officers and loggers talking in a knot near the slasher.

"Those guys tricked us, eh? Got us onto the highway." Robert's hands push into the pockets of his jacket. "But if we stick with the truth, we'll win."

I am surprised by the gracefulness of Robert's assessment. "They lied to you," I remark.

"We don't really have a word for lying in Anishinaabe. The closest we have is *gii waa ni mo wuk,* which means someone has made a mistake in their words."

12:30 A.M. Aftermath. After a fourteen-hour volley of words, the drivers decide to accept the community's original offer. They turn around.

This was a long day for the loggers (in the cabs of their machines, scheming on their CB radios), as well as for the blockaders. We ate cold, damp spaghetti from foil pans off the tailgate of a Chevy, and beans heated in the creosote fire. Someone threw lengths of an old hydro pole on the flames, and the treated wood released its chemicals into our nostrils and aching brains. Everyone is exhausted. The police go home first, then the truckers, and finally the teachers, trappers, and CPTers.

Older Brothers and Sisters

Obviously, the blockades have become a rallying point for the Grassy Narrows community, environmentalists, and other First Nations. But I sometimes wonder, Where is it going? All winter our team charted the politics of the region on the papery, cheap paneling of our rented trailer, looking for a key to a campaign that would let people across North America participate in the action of one small northern community. We did not find one. Every time I think I've understood what is taking place in Grassy Narrows, I find myself in the dark again.

CPTers from across Canada and the United States arrive intermittently at Slant Lake. Confronted with the silence of the boreal forest—with no TV, electricity, or signboard protests to keep us busy—we grasp for something "to do." Do we fail to understand the quiet power of people simply claiming their right to control their own lives? Band members are moving off the reserve, out from under Indian Affairs, back onto their land. They ask no one's permission. They petition no government to allow it. They simply point to the treaty.

A visiting chief passed through Grassy Narrows territory some time ago. Traveling in his company was a very old white man. The chief introduced himself, then motioned toward his companion: "This is my younger brother."

Our Anishinaabe hosts care for our needs, inviting us into their homes for moose meat dinners and fish fries. They speak of how they feel responsible for the nonnative people, the newcomers to this continent—their younger brothers and sisters.

During the Segise Road incident, Steve and I spoke on the satellite phone to newspapers, radio reporters, and news services all afternoon. Confused, they kept asking, "So the natives are blocking loggers from leaving the forest?" I asked community members how to answer the question. I was stumped. High-school teacher Charles Wagamese braced himself on the highway, where the dotted center line would be if there weren't an inch of ice and snow covering the road.

"They don't understand why we are here," he says. "They don't realize that they are repeating the rape of Brazil's rainforests again, that here they are tearing down the lungs of the earth and chipping them into newsprint. They don't see that this is cultural genocide.

"But the Anishinaabe—we have a responsibility to defend the treaty, the land and the children. Everyone's children! We are standing up for everyone!"

Blueberries, Rubber Boots, and Boat Rammings

Matthew Bailey-Dick

Every day there are blueberries—small ones that grow wild and close to the ground. Once in a while as I walk back to our camp-site, I forget that there are hundreds of wee berries ripening all around. Usually, though, I notice them. I stoop to marvel at their abundance and their sweet, sweet taste in my mouth. Here along the shores of Miramichi Bay and beneath the warm August sunlight, these blueberries thrive. They are well rooted and they give me grounding when everything else seems to be in turmoil.

It was only a few days ago that my wife, Nina, and I arrived in Esgenoôpetitj (Burnt Church, New Brunswick, Canada). We had come trundling along with the rented camping trailer that will serve as home base for our CPT team over the next few months. We'd been invited to camp behind the home of Isabel (one of the matriarchs of the community).

As we hastily set up the campsite—finding a place to park the trailer, figuring out a convenient source of potable water, digging a new hole for the outhouse, organizing our CPT paraphernalia —the blueberries continue their ceaseless task of growing, ripening, and becoming ever more rooted in God's good earth. They make me think of the groundedness and determination of the people of Esgenoôpetitj, and they remind me of the impor-tance of listening.

This morning I've left the campsite to take a walk on the wharf. The sun is shining brightly, though the wind seems to get stronger and the air cooler as I walk along the wooden planks extending from the shoreline. The wharf offers a good view of the community of Esgenoôpetitj and, somehow, a good perspective of what has led me to this place.

Before arriving here a few days ago, I wasn't sure what to expect in terms of "getting in the way" of violence. The CPT training Nina and I had received included a significant anti-racism component. Our CPT Ontario group had worked with several native communities as they asserted their rights and tried to counter the discrimination and violence they experienced. Now all of this training comes into play as we figure out what it means for Christians to follow God's peacemaking call into the highly charged arena of native rights and treaty relationships between Canada and First Nations peoples. I know my own identity as a white person is significant. "Getting in the way" must be both an outward task of nonviolent action as well as an inward journey through which I wrestle with the privileges I enjoy as a white person.

I knew little about the particular situation in Esgenoôpetitj First Nation (EFN) until the fall of 1999, when I began to hear radio reports about something called the "Marshall decision." This was a legal decision in which the Canadian Supreme Court affirmed that a Mi'kmaq fisher named Donald Marshall had the right to fish and earn a moderate livelihood in accordance with long-standing native traditions secured by treaties signed in the 1760s.

Then came reports in October 1999 that members of the nonnative community in Burnt Church had cut the lines of hundreds of lobster traps that had been set by the native fishers. Some nonnatives reportedly assaulted members of the native community with baseball bats. Apparently, the Royal Canadian Mounted Police (RCMP) did little to hold anyone accountable for the destruction of traps or the violence. Interestingly, a report surfaced at that time about a local nonnative pastor who stood on the wharf trying to convince some of his parishioners to stop vandalizing the lobster-fishing equipment.

In our regular CPT Ontario meetings, I listened to CPTers

who came back from Esgenoôpetitj with reports of Canadian fishery officers using their large boats to intimidate First Nations fishers. There were accounts of native fishers being charged with illegal fishing, and stories of CPTers being charged with obstruction simply for being present and operating video cameras.

A few months later, I decided to go to Esgenoôpetitj. Nina had come in the spring, and the stories of her experiences contributed to my decision. A passion for peacemaking and concern for aboriginal justice also compelled me to go. At a deeper and more mysterious level, it was a step of faith. I trusted that it was the right thing to do and that any other commitments could be put on hold for the sake of something more important. Still, I didn't know what I was getting myself into.

I'm now wearing the red CPT hat and living where the dramatic events of Esgenoôpetitj took place. The once nameless members of the native community seen in media reports are people I've now met. When I stand on the wharf, I can see their houses along a shoreline that stretches several kilometers to the horizon. I think about how this is their life—this is their story, to be told in the language of Mi'kmaq, in a place called Esgenoôpetitj. It is not a story to be told in English in a place called Burnt Church.

I realize that our first act of peacemaking must be to listen. I realize, too, that we must convey to our North American sisters and brothers that violence is not only happening "out there," in places like Hebron and Bogotá, but right here in our own land.

Standing at the end of the wharf, I use my binoculars to look at two fishers who are taking lobster traps out into the bay. They maneuver their small aluminum dory through the choppy waters and haul their lobster traps over the side of the boat with ease, in spite of the fact that each trap is weighted with a hefty concrete slab so it will sink properly. There is a particular way of baiting and setting the traps, and these fishers know what they are doing. Lobster fishing is part of the identity of the Mi'kmaq people; they are long-time conservationists who have fished during this season for thousands of years.

Yet the Canadian government and its Department of Fisheries and Oceans (DFO)—working on my behalf as a Canadian—claim that these fishers are engaging in illegal activity by fishing for lobster this time of year. The people of Esgenoôpetitj continue their centuries-old tradition of a fall lobster-fishing season. To witness the community asserting itself in this way is an exciting opportunity. But I wonder if the DFO could also see it as an opportunity to learn from this community's conservation management plan.

As I start walking back toward the shore, I think about some of the questions people asked me before I left home: So, why are you going to the east coast? What is CPT doing out there? Are you planning to be mediators? To these questions I usually respond by saying something about Esgenoôpetitj's invitation to CPT to come as peacemakers and human-rights observers. I try to explain how there are issues of structural violence and racism in Canada to which we as Christians must respond.

Would Jesus have worn hip-waders when he went into a fishing boat with his disciples? I'm not sure, but I know that following in the footsteps of the Prince of Peace means that I must be ready with a pair of sturdy rubber boots. Yesterday I hid my boots under a bush near the shore and used a thick, black marker to write my name in them so they wouldn't get mixed up with the many pairs used each day by members of the Esgenoôpetitj community. When I put on these boots I feel as if I can walk through anything; I can face any trial or tribulation. But this impression fades quickly when the action of walking—or rather clomping—forces my socks to slip down inside the boots, leaving at least the ankles bare and susceptible to rubber burn. Nevertheless, the boots are essential for participation in this CPT project site. One never knows when fishers might request a CPTer to accompany them, and the ability to leap into a boat as an observer should not be hampered by inadequate footwear.

A sturdy pair of rubber boots is just one of the essential tools for our work in Esgenoôpetitj; other tools and skills are necessary in this CPT project. We learn to cook fine cuisine on a camp stove, to operate a digital camera and a high-tech pair of binoculars (donated to CPT by a group of nuns), to determine who forgot to plug the cellular phone into the charger, and to sporadically haul a five-gallon jug of water from a nearby house to the campsite so we can brush our teeth and wash our dirty dishes. When a situation arises that merits media coverage, one of our most important tools is the laptop computer. Spending an hour or so hunched over the keyboard of the laptop can result in a press release that gets the word out to dozens of media contacts and hundreds of CPT supporters across North America. Aside from these various gizmos, our work also relies on intangibles, like the patience to make decisions by consensus within the CPT team, enthusiasm and creativity for nonviolent public witness, and a readiness to be interviewed by the media at the drop of a hat.

It also helps to be a little "crazy," as our more gracious detractors would put it. This comes in handy when it's time, for example, to hold a highly politicized worship service on the wharf in Neguac, a nonnative community close to Esgenoôpetitj, where our prayers and songs are punctuated with the curses of nonnatives who would prefer we butt out of what they see as a local problem. Or when we use scrap lumber to fashion a larger-than-life lobster trap, then take it to the local federal fisheries office and hold a service of social exorcism, praying for the spirits of greed and racism to depart from the DFO. The media are invited to watch as we put a mock "DFO officer" into the lobster trap, symbolizing how nonnatives are trapped in a certain mindset and a certain way of relating to our First Nations sisters and brothers. Of course, this is not so much craziness as boldness—a response to the daring work that God is already doing to transform hearts and build new bridges.

Sometimes when I sit around our campfire at night, I marvel at the impact of our little peacemakers' camp. Then I think about how the community of Esgenoôpetitj keeps going with so few resources. It must seem like all of Canada is against them and trying to push them off their land. I am filled with questions: What does it mean to accompany this native community as they assert their rights? Does our modest campsite mean that we are more or less respectful to the realities they deal with all the time?

These questions bring me back to my boots. One of the realizations is that this kind of peacemaking lands me deep in the muck, where I need good footwear in order to wade through the ambiguities and questions before me. Some of the muck I am faced with in Esgenoôpetitj consists of our own limitations and ignorance as whites working alongside a native community. When we fail to see our own racism or when we fail to acknowledge our own assumptions about what peacemaking should look like, we create a muddle and are unsure how to proceed. When we don't listen to the people of Esgenoôpetitj, we become clumsy and blind in our work. When we miss our daily team worship, we lose focus. Though we have our CPT tools of the trade, more significant is the way we are being "tooled" by the Creator for the work of peacemaking. A biblical word of encouragement comes to mind: "As shoes for your feet put on whatever will make you ready to proclaim the gospel of peace" (Ephesians 6:15).

The last few days have been tiring. The nearby DFO detachment in Neguac has been randomly dispatching patrols in Miramichi Bay. A couple of days ago, DFO boats arrived while it was still dark, with no navigation lights on, and began seizing dozens of EFN lobster traps. When members of the community went to confront the DFO, the officers pointed guns and blinding lights at the native fishers. That night the EFN community set up a roadblock on Highway 11, a main provincial thoroughfare, to call attention to the injustice.

Nina and I were up most of the night. She documented the treatment of a native man who was strangled and held in deplorable conditions by the local RCMP detachment. I was at the roadblock to document interactions with RCMP and local nonnatives. Of course, our fatigue was nothing when compared to that of community members, who live with this strain day in and day out, year-round.

At about 6:30 A.M., we received word that a group of DFO

boats was approaching. Because Nina had been up later than I, we agreed that I would go to the shore as an observer. I quickly put on my raincoat and my red CPT hat, and flung the digital camera bag and binoculars over my shoulder. As I clomped to the shore in my rubber boots, I realized both how important and how utterly bizarre is the role the people of Esgenoôpetitj have invited CPTers to play. Here I am, running off to make sure that federal fisheries employees—representing a government I helped to elect—don't hurt anyone.

I reached the shore where folks from Esgenoôpetitj were lined up watching the water. There was a lot of activity as fishers prepared their boats and shouted messages along the shoreline. A number of the community's conservation officers, referred to as "guardians" or "rangers," had also set out from shore. I looked through the binoculars and saw about eight or nine DFO boats coming toward the main fishing zone, where the lobster traps had been set. Suddenly, someone shouted, "Look! They're cutting traps. The DFO are cutting traps!"

Then I heard, "They need a CPTer in that boat. Come on!" So I headed toward one of the ranger boats poised to set out from shore. I stood on a rock about four feet away and three feet above the water level, unsure how to get into the boat. Someone encouraged me to jump, so I took a flying leap. Suddenly, I was sitting with four others in a motorboat as it sped away from the shore. With my hands gripping the seat and my red CPT hat lowered against the wind, I realized this was my first boat ride in Esgenoôpetitj. My ears strained to hear what the others in the boat were saying. Every once in a while, a message came through on a hand-held walkie-talkie, and one of them switched from English to Mi'kmaq to communicate with rangers in other boats.

We approached one of the DFO boats and a familiar scenario unfolded: DFO officers claimed they are patrolling the waters in order to enforce Canadian fishing rules; native men reminded the officers that they were in First Nations waters and the people of Esgenoôpetitj had a treaty right to fish for lobster. My role was to observe and, I hope, prevent violence with the camera I had ready. By now, most officers knew we distributed photos and press releases of our violence-reduction work.

I noticed that the pilot of the DFO boat is Louis Breault, an officer whose disrespect for the native community members and whose unsafe conduct on the water has been documented on CPT videos.

Suddenly, the DFO boat came toward us and rammed into the side of our vessel. "What on earth?!" I thought. "We're actually being rammed!" I had heard of other incidents in which DFO boats nearly capsized EFN boats. Still, I was amazed that it was actually happening.

The next few seconds were filled with confusion as I attempted to take photographs of the DFO boat with the digital camera and keep a firm hold of my seat so I didn't get thrown over the side. I noticed that a DFO officer who had been filming us with a video camera was no longer filming. Breault shouted at us, "Get the hell out of here!" At this point, I realized the inadequacy of a digital camera. How was I supposed to document any of this with still photos? But I kept taking pictures and struggled to change the camera's disk.

Our boat was rammed again. The DFO boat was about twice the size of ours, so we were severely jolted. It took real effort to hold on to the seat. As our boat circled away for the second time, I found myself pointing a finger at the DFO boat—right at Louis Breault himself. A single word emerged from a place of anger deep inside of me, and I spoke out loud, "You!" but without enough volume to be heard by anyone over the roar of the motors. It was a spontaneous accusing of the DFO, which made the trouble even as it claimed that the native community is the problem.

I quickly retracted my finger, fearing that my gesture might be misinterpreted in some way. I am supposed to be an observer; I'm not here to speak for the Esgenoôpetitj community. One of the DFO officers said that we were all under arrest and instructed us to return to shore. The rangers responded by saying that their job is to patrol the waters and that the people of Esgenoôpetitj have the right to be out here.

The DFO boat maintained a close proximity to ours, then rammed us one last time from behind. The impact damaged the motor and pushed our boat through the water for about seven or eight seconds. It was impossible to steer. When the DFO boat pulled back again, one of the men in our boat scrambled to the motor, where he desperately pushed and pulled on something and tried to get us moving again. Finally, our pilot gained control and we were on the way back to shore at full speed. The DFO boat chased us until the water was too shallow for its larger, deeper propeller.

At the shore, I clambered out of the boat and onto dry land. My heart was racing. As I returned to our campsite to get more blank disks for the digital camera, a radio reporter followed me with a microphone and asked me what had just happened. I attempted to give a succinct account, but as the words fell out of my mouth—"I was just in a boat that was rammed by the DFO, and they hit us three times"—I found myself flustered and distracted. I couldn't focus on the questions. Then she was gone.

I wound up back at the shore again, with a different camera in hand. Somebody motioned me toward another boat and said they wanted a CPTer to come with them. I jumped into this second boat and was again speeding away from the shore. During this second ride, I had a chance to photograph a number of DFO boats as they probed through the morning fog. Some were grey "shark" boats like the one driven by Breault; some were white speedboats; some were large, red Coast Guard vessels. I wondered if any of these officers were enjoying themselves. Was this just a job for them—all in a day's work? What are their families like? What would happen if we were to sit down at the same supper table tonight? How can we find a way of really understanding each other?

The situation had been covered in the press in recent weeks as everyone waited to see whether the people of Esgenoôpetitj would actually "defy the Canadian government" and bait their lobster traps. Now that an outright confrontation had occurred on the water, several television stations arrived with large satellite-transmission trucks, and reporters gathered along the shore. Evidently, we were in the midst of a national media event.

For the next two days, several national television networks asked me in interviews to describe my experience of being on a boat rammed by the DFO. I became familiar with the special microphones they fed up through my shirt and the tiny hidden earpiece through which I could hear questions posed by the anchorperson in Toronto. I was glad the television viewers could only see and hear me, because I hadn't showered for days.

The interviews were exhausting and involved a great deal of pressure to speak articulately and concisely. Some of the interviewers were matter-of-fact and respectful. Others conveyed the impression that it would take a complete fool to believe anything I had to say. I tried to keep in mind something we learned in the media segment of our CPT training: if you cannot answer or don't like a question you are asked in an interview, unapologetically answer a different question.

When several interviewers insinuated that I must be "losing my neutrality" by going in a boat with native people, I tried to explain that it was not possible to be neutral in a situation of injustice. I also tried to draw attention to the larger issue of the need for a dialogue between the people of Esgenoôpetitj and the Canadian government.

After the cameras and microphones were turned off, I walked back to our campsite, wondering how the story would be conveyed over the airwaves. *When will they interview one of the native men who were on the boat?* I realized the extent to which my white skin and my identity as a man carried an invisible though powerful message: this person is important, believable, and should be interviewed. It felt counterproductive to me to be working against racism, raising awareness about treaty rights, and standing with First Nations peoples, while at the same time perpetuating that very same racism by speaking as "the authoritative white person." The four other men who were in the boat could have provided a compelling account of the boat ramming and could have spoken more authoritatively about the issues.

Was this a case of CPTers using our white privilege as a tool for dismantling that same privilege? The national news media weren't taking the time to explore such questions.

The flock of media people with their telephoto lenses and real-time satellite links did not seem to stop the DFO's aggressive tactics. The situation became even more disturbing over the next week as other native boats were rammed and even capsized

Canadian Department of Fisheries and Oceans officer Louis Breault pursues the boat of Mi'kmaq lobster fishers.

by DFO vessels. Fishers were knocked off their boats, pepper-sprayed while in the water, and then arrested for obstruction of an officer. When asked by the media to justify the boat rammings, a DFO spokesperson said that they could have been the result of "mechanical failure." The DFO deployed a helicopter and a large (and very loud) plane that repeatedly flew low along the shoreline. Most absurd was the arrival of RCMP zodiac boats, used to transport teams of police officers in riot gear, each with a machine gun. Was this kind of violence and intimidation supposed to happen in the multicultural and peaceable nation of Canada?

Every once in a while, I received a glimmer of hope. A phone call from CPT Canada coordinator Doug Pritchard filled me with strength. He talked about how CPT supporters across North America were praying for our team in Esgenoôpetitj and about how the situation was being followed across Canada in the news. I was uplifted when native and nonnative people expressed support to the people of Esgenoôpetitj.

Our CPT team was invited to a pow-wow, where we feasted

on lobster, observed traditional Mi'kmaq dancing, and listened as community members expressed a desire to continue the struggle. Our team's worship times also gave me strength. The small circle of CPTers sang and prayed together in a way that bolstered my faith and challenged me to see God's much larger project of peace and redemption.

Two years later, I am sitting in the basement of a courthouse in Miramichi as a witness in the trial pertaining to this boat-ramming incident. Ironically, the native man who was driving our boat at the time it was rammed by the DFO has been charged with dangerous driving. The defense lawyer explains that all I need to do is describe what happened in my own words. This is what I hope to do. I pray that God will calm me and make it easy for me to speak clearly and convincingly about my experience. Upstairs Nina sits in the courtroom with our four-month-old son, Foster. Their presence also calms me.

While waiting to be called upstairs to testify, I sit with two of the native men who were on the boat with me that day. I haven't seen them since the incident. They tell stories about the many economic problems their community has faced. The DFO has had a history of conflict with native communities on the east coast, they say, and Canadians do not understand the extent of racism toward native people. One of the men describes how he was injured in the boat ramming. He still takes prescription painkillers every day for leg and back pain. In another part of the basement, I hear DFO officers talking as they prepare their testimony. The experience is somewhat profound: the physical separation in the courtroom basement begins to resemble the rift between the native community and the Canadian government. It is symbolic of broader realities: The need for real communication is still apparent.

After waiting for hours, I'm called to the courtroom. The formal atmosphere seems stiff and contrived. But I go in the trust that the Holy Spirit will help me to "speak truth to power." Unfortunately, truth is opaque in some courts of law. The prosecuting attorney aggressively cross-examines me. He's trying to trick me into contradicting myself. But after rehashing the story again and again, I am dismissed with "no further questions." Court is adjourned for the day, and because I have a plane to catch, I will not be returning for the conclusion of the trial.

I later find out that our boat driver was found guilty.

This is likely my last time in Esgenoôpetitj for a while. Nina and I have reconnected with people in the community and learned what might be happening with the fishery in the coming year. Unfortunately, it seems that nothing has been resolved regarding treaty rights and the need for new conversation between the Canadian government and the leadership of Esgenoôpetitj.

Will we be invited back again to accompany this community? Now that we've built relationships with specific people in Esgenoôpetitj, how will we stay connected? On a more personal level, how will I return home and share my experiences in a way that respects the lives and struggles of this First Nations community?

Before leaving the community, we walk around our old CPT campsite and visit with Isabel and some of her family. While there, one of Isabel's granddaughters holds Foster, and I am captivated by the two of them together. It's not the "cuteness factor" that grabs me. It's the impossible being stripped away to reveal a future in which these two might live together more fully as sister and brother. It's the kindling of some kind of relentless hope in the middle of a long and hard journey.

As we walk back to our rental car, I glance down at the ground and notice the wild blueberry bushes continuing their silent vigil over Miramichi Bay. It's been almost a month since they stopped producing. For this year.

Standing in the Gap

Mark Frey

As we go over our team roles in preparation for the march, the streets outside CPT's Hebron apartment are quiet. Not one Palestinian is in the market, the center of economic life in the Old City. A twenty-four hour curfew has been saddled on the thirty thousand Palestinians living in H2, the 20 percent of Hebron under Israeli military control. For Palestinians to go outside their homes means possible arrest. In some cases, they might be shot.

The present curfew was imposed after Palestinian gunmen sprayed automatic rifle fire at a Jewish settler van. Two women were injured. They were among the four hundred fundamentalist Jews who live in the midst of this Palestinian city of 140,000. The curfew applies only to the Palestinians in H2 and is seen by them as collective punishment. But the Israelis view it as a security measure, and the settlers who live just a few doors away from the CPT apartment are permitted to move freely. As international observers, so are we.

It is early Sunday morning, January 10, 1999. Curfew is unusual at this hour. We're unaccustomed to the eerie quiet and nervous as we go through our checklist: "Who's taking pictures?" "Who's on arrest support?" Uniform: red hat, red armband—check. Equipment: passports, cell-phones, cameras, press list—check. Standing in a circle, we gather for a final prayer—"God be with us and guide our feet"—before we take to the silent streets. We cannot know that the day will end in dramatic fashion: we'll prevent Israeli soldiers from killing people, and two of our teammates will be jailed.

Pierre Shantz, Sara Reschly, and I have worked together in Hebron for two years, and with Joanne "Jake" Kaufman for a year. Only Sydney Stigge is new, and she is sharp. At twenty-nine, I am the oldest.

Our team has been through a lot in the past week. Five days ago, the curfew had been in effect for two days. I was awakened by shots that seemed to come from just outside our door. I threw on my clothes, and we all raced outside to see a Palestinian man lying on the ground, gasping for air. Israeli medics quickly arrived to treat the man just shot by Israeli soldiers. One said, "He was outside during curfew. He did not stop. He had a gun." Lying beside the dying body was a clear plastic, sci-fi-looking ray gun. Was the man carrying it, or had it been placed there? We'll never know. His glassy eyes stared at nothing, and I saw his guts coming out of the bullet wound in his side. In a moment of pure dissociation, I thought, "This looks just like the movies." Sara left the scene crying. She was taken in by a Palestinian family who spoke no English, but communicated the language of compassion by offering her water and food.

Yellow incident tape was strung around the scene as a soldier tried to shoo us away. As CPTers, we're supposed to challenge military domination. Stubborn and in shock, I refused to move. The soldier looked at me and said sincerely, "Really, we're trying to help." I stepped out of the way. They rushed the man to a Jerusalem hospital, where he died. Later we learned that he was developmentally disabled. A military occupation is not a forgiving environment. It does not make accommodations.

We spent the next few days processing this event and talking about what it might be like to get shot. Sara decides that if she's shot, she hopes it will be in the arm or leg. We all know this is a dangerous place. But now we've seen that danger first hand, and I've seen my first dying man.

On this Sunday morning, though, we're hoping there won't be any shooting at the march. Our team has joined other tame, symbolic Palestinian demonstrations in H1, the 80 percent of Hebron under Palestinian control, where there are no Israeli soldiers. But we sense that this march might be different.

I'm disappointed that we've cancelled a hiking outing with other internationals. But we decided we needed a presence at the march in case "something happens." Organized by local political leaders of the Palestinian Authority, the march will directly confront Israeli soldiers by attempting to enter H2, the curfew zone, and walk to the Ibrahimi Mosque. The mosque is on one side of the Cave of Machpelah, where tradition says Abraham and Sarah are buried—a major holy site in both Judaism and Islam. During curfew, Muslims (but not Jews) are de facto barred from worshipping. The march is an assertion of the freedom to move and worship.

The Palestinian leadership is committed to keeping this confrontation nonviolent. We saw the same commitment demonstrated two days earlier, when a similar march challenged a roadblock at the city's entrance. When young Palestinian men, *shabab*, got hotheaded, the march leaders calmed them down. The Israeli soldiers, on the other hand, were unrestrained, and several times I stepped between angry soldiers and *shabab*. If things are similar today, there is a role for international violence intervention. So I'm nervous. Like most people, I don't like conflict. (Don't ask me why I joined CPT.)

I'm sweating as we walk. The day is warm, but I've worn my winter coat. Embarrassed, I don't tell my teammates why: if soldiers fire rubber-coated metal bullets, I want the extra padding. Silly me—as if a little padding will stop bullets. I know it's a psychological crutch for my nervousness.

We pass out of H2 and into H1, out of the curfew zone, and into the city that comes to bustling life as people go about their "normal" routines. Weaving around taxis and street vendors, we arrive at the Hebron Municipal Building and join the gathering crowd. The core of the group consists of older professional men in suits—not your typical demonstrators. We greet the journalists, who are local Palestinian stringers for the major news agencies. We've developed a good relationship with these reporters. Their English is good, and because they're often in the thick of things, filming and taking pictures, they're a wealth of information. They often share what they've learned with us. Many of them have been injured or beaten by Israeli soldiers, but they keep doing their jobs.

We greet Mazan Dana and Nael Shiyouki, a cameraman and a soundman for Reuters. (Tragically, Mazan would survive a journalistic career under brutal Israeli military occupation only to be killed at age forty-three by U.S. occupation forces in Baghdad in 2003. A soldier atop a tank fired a machine gun at him, thinking his camera looked like a shoulder-fired, rocket-propelled grenade. It was two days before Mazan's scheduled return to Hebron.)

The march gets underway. As if to emphasize the nonviolent nature of the gathering, small children lead the crowd, holding pictures of political leaders assassinated by the Israelis. Journalists run ahead to take pictures. Onlookers join to see what might happen. The leadership of the march is committed to nonviolence, but some *shabab* seem to be itching for a chance to throw stones at Israeli soldiers. The route will cross into the H2 curfew area at the junction where near-daily clashes have erupted. When *shabab* surreptitiously pick up stones in preparation, the leaders yell at them, "*Walla hajar!*"—"Not one stone!" One leader angrily rips stones out of hands. They're working hard to keep things nonviolent.

As we near the clash point, Sara and Pierre see an opportunity

CPTer Sara Reschly helps block soldiers from firing at Palestinians during a nonviolent march.

to prepare the soldiers by telling them that the marchers aren't throwing stones. Sara quickly finds our red hats in the crowd and yells, "We're running ahead to tell the soldiers." Usually, the troops take cover behind four-foot-wide cement blocks to shoot at the stone-throwers. But the soldiers aren't there. Maybe they have orders to let the march pass.

But just as the march reaches the border, a squad of soldiers charges down the alley, garbed in full riot gear: plastic shields, face plates, tear gas, grenades, and assault rifles. They move into firing positions. Pierre, Sara, and at least one Palestinian man leap in front of the leveled M-16s, screaming "Don't shoot! This is nonviolent! They're not throwing stones!" They're trying to use their whole bodies to stop more death. CPTers run to the front of the crowd and do the same. If the soldiers are going to fire, they will shoot us first, and we're banking they won't.

Although I'm in the center of the scene, I'm aware of the high drama. This is good stuff, and the journalists are snapping pictures and filming. The images of Sara and Pierre with arms waving in the air will be sent around the world: "Peacemakers stop Israeli troops in Hebron."

Having an M-16 pointed at one's belly is a frightening and profound experience, but the proximity works in one's favor. It's one thing for soldiers to shoot faceless targets at a distance; it's another for them to shoot someone looking them in the eye. I know the soldier in front of me. He's probably ten years younger than I. We've had run-ins with him before. He's abusive—what Pierre calls a "jerky boy"—and he's frustrated that he cannot fire into the crowd, just meters away. He yells, "Go! Get out of the way!" I have no doubt that, if not for us, he and the others would fire at close range and very likely kill the children at the front of the crowd. Instead, he and the others lob four percussion grenades into the crowd—mini-bombs designed for "crowd control." They explode with a deafening bang and flame. I cringe at the explosion. My eardrums hurt, and I can't hear for several minutes. The grenade casings blow in all directions and a piece hits me in the arm, leaving an ugly bruise. I'm glad now that I've worn my padded winter coat. One Palestinian youth, closer to the explosion, suffers major burns on his back.

The Palestinian leadership scrambles to regain control of the scattered crowd. "No stones! No stones!" they yell. Now the *shabab* desperately want to respond to the grenades, but they obey the march leaders. The crowd advances meters into the curfew zone, where soldiers line up, shield to shield, to prevent a further incursion. The standoff begins: a line of young soldiers itching to shoot, the Palestinian crowd with young *shabab* itching to throw stones, and five CPTers in the middle. The march leaders start "negotiations" with the older soldiers. The yelling, arguing, and talking is part of vying for space and is intrinsic to these demonstrations. The officers are not going to let the marchers continue, but they can stay for the time being.

I'm almost incapacitated by how volatile the situation is. What are we North Americans doing here? The young adults on both sides want to rumble, while the leaders on both sides try to negotiate something other than violence. Locked in conflict, each side mirrors the other. Perhaps it's a metaphor for the larger peace process.

After twenty minutes, a fed-up soldier takes it upon himself to move things forward and plows into the crowd, shoving Palestinians back with his plastic body shield. The crowd surges back. The *shabab* whoop and holler as if to say, "Bring it on." Palestinian leaders scurry to control the crowd: "No stones!" The soldiers, trained for combat and not for police-like engagements with crowds, instinctively take up firing positions. We CPTers again position ourselves in front of the guns. "Don't shoot!" we scream. An Israeli officer physically yanks back his hotheads. Thank God for mature leadership on both sides. Without it, the encounter would surely degenerate into chaos. Only four stones have been thrown, without injury.

The crowd returns and the standoff resumes. An Israeli border police commander, one of the regional higher-ups, is enraged. We have twice interfered with his troops and prevented them from carrying out orders. He starts screaming at Pierre, his face inches away, spittle coming out of his mouth. Almost as animated, but without the rage, Pierre screams back, "Keep your soldiers under control! This is nonviolent!" Unaccustomed to having someone talk back to him, the officer slaps Pierre smartly three times on the cheek. Pierre, a little stunned, yells back, "That's going in the report!" I smile. We will definitely write that in our report.

The officer turns on me and continues screaming. He is gesturing wildly and ordering me to leave. I'm unaware if he's shouting in Hebrew or English; I have tuned him out. My natural response is different from Pierre's—I just stand there and let him rage. He only gets angrier. Soon a few Palestinians come up behind me and gently pull me back, encouraging me to stand down. They are right. Stepping back a few feet allows him to save face and de-escalates the situation. My stubbornness is not an asset.

Israeli civilian police arrive on the scene. The border police commander fingers Pierre. The police grab him by the arm and march him off to the jeep. Sara demands to know why Pierre is being arrested, and the commander decrees, "Arrest her too!" Hmmm. We quickly realize that our red hats, which we use to help us find each other in a crowd, are also clear identifiers for the police. We'd all intervened and might all be arrested. I take off my hat and red armband and fade into the crowd while still keeping an eye on Joanne and Sydney at the front. I am on arrest support, which means at all costs I am to avoid arrest, so that at least one person can call lawyers, supporters, media, and the Chicago office. (When internationals are arrested it's by civilian, not military, police. Palestinians are living under Israeli military occupation. They are, therefore, under military law and go to military court. Internationals and Israelis in the West Bank benefit from being classified differently. They fall within Israeli civilian law, which is much nicer.)

Pierre and Sara are taken away. Soldiers detain Sydney and Joanne, but they are released shortly. They continue to strategically place themselves between Palestinians and soldiers, at times chastising the young Israelis for continuing to point their assault rifles at the mingling crowd. It is hard for soldiers to hear this kind of disapproval from women.

The tense standoff is effectively managed by the march leaders and, in particular, one Israeli Druze officer, who speaks Arabic and proves to be very reasonable. When a Palestinian complains that a soldier is pointing a rifle at the marchers, the officer pushes the gun aside.

But I'm getting nervous. One stone can break this delicate balance. The longer we stand still, the greater the potential for a blow-up. After more than an hour, the soldiers and crowd are growing restless.

Inevitably, the *shabab* start whooping, and it looks like stones will fly. In a brilliant move, the leaders preempt the violence by calling for everyone to pray in the street. Out come prayer rugs—from where, I don't know. Some find pieces of cardboard from the market vegetable stalls. The leaders kneel down to pray in rows. Impressive. They've clearly thought this through. The Druze officer, understanding the tactic, circulates among the *shabab* and encourages them to join in prayer. Some are smiling sheepishly, not knowing how to respond to an Israeli officer encouraging them to pray.

After the prayer, the leaders declare the march over. One comes to me and thanks CPT for its contribution. The leaders depart, leaving *shabab* and soldiers to mingle. In my mind, it's a recipe for disaster. The three of us CPTers caucus and decide to leave too. Our reasoning: we are there to stop soldiers from attacking a nonviolent demonstration; we are not there to stop soldiers from shooting at stone-throwing *shabab*. We are surprised to learn later that clashes did not break out, though the crowd remained for some time.

We are euphoric. We jumped in front of the guns and enacted archetypal violence reduction. Back at the apartment, we begin our follow-up: calling our Israeli partners, the media, and CPT's Chicago office, writing press releases, and locating Sara and Pierre.

Sara is released after five hours because there are no facilities for women at the police substation in Hebron. She is ordered to return at eight the next morning. Pierre, however, is detained overnight. The pair is eventually scheduled to appear in a Jerusalem court at noon. After Sara informs us, we call our lawyers and other supporters.

At the courthouse in Jerusalem, we greet Sara and Pierre, along with a collection of journalists and an array of more than twenty supporters—mostly internationals and Israelis, including one rabbi and two children. The kids have been pulled out of school for the day by their mother, a friend of the team, who does not want her children to miss this moment. Sara and Pierre smile as they pass through metal detectors. Pierre is still wearing shackles and cuffs, but Sara is unfettered. One of the children exclaims, "Look, Mom, Pierre has no shoelaces!"

As they shuffle from room to room with their entourage in tow, Sara and Pierre's presence creates a commotion. Some lawyers in the hall ask what has happened. When told, some express appreciation.

With Sara and Pierre in the dock, CPT lawyer Jonathan Kuttab addresses the court in Hebrew. His remarks are barely comprehensible to us. But I can read body language, and the police are not winning. Our Israeli friends translate. The officers request that Sara and Pierre be barred from Hebron for fifteen days. "Denied," the judge says, on the grounds that the case is not sufficiently strong. The judge allows the investigation to continue for an additional three weeks, after which the case will be closed. Bail is set at two thousand shekels each (about one thousand U.S. dollars total), which we raise immediately from our supporters.

I admire Pierre and Sara for their courage. They've been arrested as we've accomplished something good, something life-affirming. Although he's quite a bit younger than I, Pierre is like the brother I look up to. And Sara . . . I cannot know at the time that we'll get married three years later.

We pass the police in the hall and Jonathan jokes, "You're free to go now," expressing the levity and triumph we all feel. One officer turns, seriousness on his brow, "This is a court of law, not a theater."

Pierre and Sara give interviews to the waiting journalists. "How can you defend this?" asks a disapproving Israeli Associated Press camera operator, who speaks with a thick Hebrew accent. "What's to stop you from doing this all over the West Bank?"

He senses the fundamental danger our nonviolent resistance poses to the occupation. What is to stop us? "Only our fear," I think to myself. Only our fear.

Witnessing Demolition, Fasting for Rebuilding

Dianne Roe

I will never forget the day the Israeli military bulldozed the home of Waheed Zalloum in late February 1996. I had just completed Christian Peacemaker Teams training in Chicago in January and had been in Hebron only a few weeks. Word reached us that Israeli occupation forces were demolishing twenty homes in the hills of Hebron. "Could you go there?" Israeli friends in Jerusalem asked. We grabbed our backpacks, not knowing exactly where we were going.

An hour or so later, I waited along with CPTers Kathy Kern, Anne Montgomery, and Bob Naiman for the convoy of Israeli army bulldozers. We were on the rooftop of the house of Waheed Zalloum. My teammate Cole Hull passed a video camera up to me. I saw Manal Zalloum hold her baby and weep. I wept with her and panned the area around the fertile valley called Wadi Ghuruus. Children waited with anxious faces in the nearby vineyard. A few hundred yards south of the vineyard, I could see the red rooftops in the Israeli settlement of Kiryat Arba. An Israeli military camp spanned the valley and connected Kiryat Arba to Givat Harsina, another Israeli settlement to the north.

I saw the bulldozers approach. What chance did these families have against an occupation army? What could they do, surrounded by enemies who wanted their land?

The scenes that followed have remained with me. The soldiers roughed up Bob as they removed us from the roof. We watched in horror as a bulldozer smashed into the house. Women screamed and children wept as they saw the home smashed to the ground. Bob and I were arrested for refusing to leave a closed military zone.

In a Jerusalem jail cell during the days that followed, I tried to communicate with my Israeli cellmates what I had witnessed. But they were recent immigrants from the former Soviet Union who had been arrested for prostitution, and they spoke little English. I was left with only my thoughts. Was there anything we could have done to stop the demolition? How could we prevent more demolitions? Would the Israeli authorities deport me?

I later learned that in the hours following the demolitions, the CPT office was very busy. Supporters from many corners of the world sent faxes to Israeli officials on behalf of Bob and me. Five days later, he and I waited with our lawyer, Allegra Pacheko, for a court hearing. I feared deportation. "Only two weeks on assignment," I thought, "and it could end right now." Then, by some kind of miracle, Allegra announced that we were free to go because the police bringing charges against us did not show up. We celebrated our release, though our celebration was bittersweet. The Zalloum house was still a pile of ruins.

Slated for Demolition

A month later, the fields were muddy from the spring rains when Anne, Bob, and I trudged up the winding road from Hebron's Old City toward Wadi Ghuruus and the Beqa'a Valley —the most fertile farmland in Hebron.

We had with us a list of ten families whose houses were slated for demolition. According to the Hebron municipality that gave us the list, each family had been ordered by the Israeli Civil Administration to demolish their home by May 1. If they refused, the Israeli military would do it for them and send them the bill for the bulldozer. The deadline was a month away.

We passed the demolished Zalloum home and met Salah Jaber along the path. He spoke a little English and said he would introduce us to some other people. As we went looking for the home of Ata Jaber, Salah pointed out four other demolished homes along the dirt road, all of which had been destroyed the same day as the Zalloum's. He told us that most of the homes on the list were located near the new road the locals called *sharia jideed* (Arabic for "new road"). In 1995, the Israeli Civil Administration had begun building a system of bypass roads designed to allow Israeli settlers to travel to Jerusalem without passing through Palestinian towns. *Sharia jideed* was the reason Palestinian homes were being demolished. No Palestinian families with land near the road's planned path were given building permits.

The road cut through the fields of the Jaber families. The cave at the back had been the family dwelling for generations. Ata Jaber and his brothers had tried many times to get a permit to build a house or even to add on to their father's existing house. But the civil administration routinely denied them the right to build on their own land.

Ata was not home, but we met his wife, Rodeina, who was holding infant Dahlia. Amoona, a toddler, nestled up against her on the cement floor. We sat on mattresses on the floor and sipped tea. I spoke no Arabic, and Rodeina spoke no English. But I thought, "Everyone knows baby talk." So, trying to ease the obvious distress I read on the faces of Rodeina and her children, I tried the baby-talk approach. I held the infant Dahlia and remarked how beautiful she was.

Salah asked Rodeina to explain the situation with the demolition order. I videotaped the interview and hoped to someday understand what Rodeina was saying.

In the following weeks, we learned of sixty houses in the Hebron hills ordered demolished. In early April, CPTer Wendy Lehman, Anne, and I witnessed six demolitions near the Jaber home. We cried with the families and tried to meet more of the families whose homes were threatened.

Kathy Kern and I came up with the idea of inviting Israelis to meet Palestinian families experiencing demolition. Aliza Zutra, an Israeli from Rehovot, said she would lead such a delegation. When her group of five committed Israeli peace activists returned home, they called their friends and sent faxes to officials, and told others to do the same.

Two days later, just one day before the May 1 deadline on the demolition order, Israeli Prime Minister Shimon Peres and Palestinian President Yasir Arafat issued a joint declaration that the sixty homes in the Hebron area would *not* be demolished.

But a month later, Benjamin Netanyahu was elected prime minister, and no one knew what might happen then.

Deciding to Fast

In February 1997, a year after we'd witnessed the bulldozing of the Zalloum house, the Israeli military started demolishing houses again. Mark Frey—just out of CPT training—joined me and team members Cliff Kindy, Art Gish, and Terry Rempel in trying to find a way to challenge the demolitions. In mid-February, we heard that seven hundred families in the West Bank were facing destruction of their homes. At the time, we were meeting regularly with a member of the Hebron Land Defense Committee, an expert cartographer for the Hebron municipality. He brought us a map of the district and pointed out the areas most vulnerable to demolition. He also offered to take us there and introduce us to some of the families.

Even in the midst of great poverty and deprivation, family after family we visited offered us cups of tea. Children peeked from behind their mothers' skirts and shyly reached out to the *ajnabiyya* (foreign woman) they saw conversing with their parents. Once again, the human face of the occupation moved us. The world has no idea what the Palestinians are experiencing. We had not known the full extent of it, and we were living in their midst. Even our most savvy Israeli friends were unaware of the reality of the occupation. It was as if the suffering of the Palestinians had become invisible.

We were being pulled in a dozen different directions. What could we do to stop the demoli-

A Palestinian woman talks with soldiers after her house was destroyed by Israeli Defense Forces during a string of home demolitions in February 1997.

tions? We could not be in seven hundred different places at once. How could we document the stories of all the effected families?

We made the decision to fast for seven hundred hours—one hour for each of the looming demolitions. We began the Fast for Rebuilding on March 1, with three team members doing a liquid-only fast and the others, a Ramadan-style fast that consisted of eating only between sundown and sunrise. During the first week of our fast, Anne and Sara joined our team and joined us in fasting.

The "success" of the fast depended on making important connections. It was crucial that we fast in public. We also would need a tent to shelter us from the rain and cold and to symbolize the homelessness caused by home demolition. (After their homes are demolished, many families are forced to live in tents.)

As we made our plans in mid-February 1997, it was just one month after implementation of the initial stages of the Hebron agreement. The agreement was part of the Oslo peace process, which had begun in September 1993 with the famous White-House-lawn handshake of Yitzhak Rabin and Yasir Arafat. In January 1997, Israeli soldiers left some areas of Hebron, while other areas remained under full occupation, including the farmland where Ata and his cousins lived. The Palestinian Authority had administrative power in only a small area of the Hebron District.

During the fast, we ended up locating our tent adjacent to the Red Cross offices in Hebron. We received an outpouring of support from many Israeli friends in Jerusalem, Bethlehem, and elsewhere. Visitors from Sabeel (a Palestinian Christian Liberation Theology organization in Jerusalem), Rabbis for Human Rights, Israelis and Palestinians for Nonviolence, and a United Methodist group in Jericho also showed their support.

From our tent, we talked with Palestinians about their lives in Hebron. We had heard about how many remote areas in the district were facing house demolitions. We couldn't visit them all, but we wondered if we could get representatives of some of these communities to visit us.

As we were planning the fast, we knew March 8 was International Woman's Day. Could we invite women in the community to hold a press conference at the tent? Could we find a woman who could express what she felt in losing her home? We met a woman named Zleekha, who introduced us to women's organizations in the community.

As news of the fast spread through our many contacts, journalists were anxious to interview us. But we had decided that it was important to keep the focus on the issue of home demolitions. To help with this, we kept a notebook at the ready and encouraged Palestinians to record their stories in it. The stories were written in Arabic and later translated into English for us to read.

We also began to build relationships with people in the area. Our tent was near a secondary school attended by boys from all around Hebron. Some of the students began to stop by after school to practice their English with us. They told us stories of their villages, and we made it a point to refer to these stories when speaking with journalists.

People from around the world told us they were joining our fast. We wrote their names on a sheet and posted it in the tent. The various delegations visiting us enlarged the scope of the fast. Cliff told us about a friend of his who was taking the fast to Washington, D.C. He set up a tent in the capitol and handed out information about Israel's policy of demolishing homes. The issue was beginning to get some exposure.

Jabers Under Threat

On the fifth day of the fast, a journalist friend stopped by our tent. He brought news that the Israeli military was demolishing homes in the Beqa'a Valley. "They are at the home of Ata Jaber, threatening to demolish," he said. A year earlier, Ata's name had been a mere scribble on a slip of paper. Now he was a close friend of our team. I recalled my visit with Rodeina and their two babies. I remembered Dahlia and the "baby talk." Now the threatening bulldozers were at their doorstep.

Anne, Mark, and I left the tent and walked through the fields to Ata's home. By the time we arrived, Cliff, Terry, Art, and Harriet Lewis, a friend and Israeli Jew, were already there. *Sharia jideed* was by then a working road, and they had taken a taxi. The family had removed their belongings from the home, and the bulldozers had left but were expected to return later in the day. Harriet and Terry went with some journalists and members of the Palestinian Land Defense Committee, who were following the bulldozers to Yatta. There, Harriet witnessed her first home demolition. She told us it changed her life.

Meanwhile, Art and I had to leave for business in Hebron. I later returned to Ata's home, bringing along Israeli and Methodist groups. When the bulldozers arrived, they drove right past the house. Ata attributed that to the presence of Israelis and internationals. His home had been spared, at least for the time being.

The next day Ata visited us at our CPT headquarters. I told him that I had met Rodeina a year earlier, when Dahlia was a baby. "I know," Ata said. He went on to tell me how the visit had looked to Rodeina. Apparently, my baby talk had not translated well, and she thought I was planning to take the baby away. I felt terrible when I heard this. I looked into Ata's face for the rebuke I knew I deserved, but I saw only forgiveness and reassurance. My baby-talk incident became a joke between our team and the Jaber family. Dahlia became our first CPT baby.

But how vulnerable these families are! I learned later about the miscarriages Rodeina had suffered from the trauma of soldiers knocking at her door. I also learned of the humiliation felt by husbands and fathers when they're unable to protect their families.

Making Connections

Two days later, women from Hebron marched through the streets and stopped in front of our fasting tent to make speeches. Local television stations covered the march, and some international press was present. The village women sitting with us in the tent provided an impressive visual image and put a very human face on the occupation.

Many of the Palestinians stopping by the tent invited us to their villages. In response, Mark and Anne went with representatives of the Hebron Land Defense Committee to photograph and document homes facing demolition near the border village of Beit Meersam. I went with a delegation to the village of Sair to get stories of demolition families in Beit Anoon, between Sair and Hebron.

Meanwhile, some Israeli groups were already galvanized on issues relating to land confiscation, settlement expansion, and home demolition. Israel was preparing to build a settlement on Jabal Abu Gneim, near Beit Sahur, and on March 18, Sara and Cliff joined other activists in a demonstration at the site.

To end our fast, we decided to return to a demolished home to plan a rebuilding. Rabbi Arik Ascherman of Rabbis for Human Rights joined us in clearing rubble at the ruins of the Zalloum home in Wadi Ghuruus, where I had been arrested a year earlier. The Israeli military detained Arik, Cliff, and two Palestinians. We didn't succeed in clearing the rubble, but important bonds were being forged between CPT and other peace workers. When we broke our fast on Easter Sunday in Jerusalem, Cliff was still detained, but he left Israel the next day, which was his scheduled departure date.

Our fast bore fruit in many ways. It sparked some important initiatives and led to the formation of lasting relationships among groups working for human rights in Palestine. Three of the Israeli activists who had supported us in our fast—Harriet, Arik, and Amos Gvirtz—helped found the Israeli Committee Against Home Demolitions (ICAHD). Harriet attributed her passion for the issue to the time she had spent with us. Witnessing a home demolition had made the occupation personal for her. One of the goals of ICAHD is to make it personal for other Israelis too. Around the time ICAHD was formed, CPT simultaneously developed the Campaign for Secure Dwellings, a program aimed at connecting North American churches and other groups with families experiencing the nightmare of home demolition.

But most important, the fast drew attention to the issue of home demolitions in the West Bank and gave voice to Palestinians who were previously unheard.

Ready to Return

As I write this account, it is seven years since our 1997 fast, and I am preparing for Lent 2004. After a break at home in New York, I'm getting ready to return to Hebron. Many of the places I visited in 1997, including the land of Waheed Zalloum and Ata Jaber, have been severely impacted by the "separation wall" that Israel is building. In the years since our fast, Ata's house has been demolished and rebuilt multiple times. Many other families have suffered the same.

Seven years after he was arrested for clearing rubble at the Zalloum ruins, Rabbi Arik Ascherman faces trial again, this time for trying to stop a home demolition in Jerusalem.

Did we succeed in putting a human face on the home demolition issue? I believe we did. Where I make my home in the Finger Lakes region of New York, people know Ata Jaber and Arik Ascherman. But the demolitions continue. The Israeli army continues to uproot families. The human face that we helped the world to see is still streaked with tears. We have, however, also experienced moments of joy in friendships across borders and separation walls. The Fast for Rebuilding succeeded in building a structure for peace between strangers, and it is a structure no wall can destroy.

Sometimes You Have to Bend So You Don't Break

Wendy Lehman

The Israeli police guard directed "Joan" and me to a ten-by-ten-foot jail cell containing bunks and three Israeli prisoners. The thin, foam mattress pads smelled of urine. The floor was streaked with black grime. The door was solid metal with a tiny, gated window, and the squat toilet was hidden by a small cement wall with no door. "Great," I thought. "Now what?"

Eighteen hours earlier that day in May 1996, my Christian Peacemaker Teams mates and I were digging up olive tree saplings that Israeli settlers had planted on land owned by "Abed," a Palestinian with whom we had worked for several months. (This tree-planting tactic is often used by Israeli settlers to claim land.) Our CPT team in Hebron was removing the trees at Abed's request. He owned land near an especially militant Israeli settlement on the outskirts of Hebron, where settlers challenged his claim to the land. His family had long depended on the income earned from farming, and he couldn't wait for the Israeli courts, which could take months or even years to resolve his dispute with the settlers. He needed to plow his land and plant his wheat, which was impossible with trees planted on it.

Joan, an American who ran a reconciliation center in Hebron, first presented Abed's case to our team. The settlers had fenced off the land in an attempt to seize it. Abed asked if we would be willing to remove the fence, because he was afraid to. In the past, Palestinians who attempted to defy neighboring settlers often faced intimidation or beatings. Even if they filed a police report, Israeli police rarely helped them. In a field near Abed's, one Palestinian was found bound and gagged, shot in the head. When we removed the fence from Abed's field, we left a note saying CPT was responsible, to protect Abed from trouble.

Removing the fence was perfectly consistent with the work our team had been doing since the Hebron project began in June 1995. We would accompany Palestinians, document human-rights abuses, report to our home churches and communities, and support locally initiated nonviolent direct action.

Our team had some apprehension about working with Joan. Our experiences with her had not always been positive. Her motives seemed to be genuine, but she often held a naïve, simplistic view of the Israeli-Palestinian conflict, and she wasn't politically savvy. Sometimes we feared Joan's approach might put people at risk—if, for example, she shared personal information about her Palestinian contacts with Israeli settlers. But we knew Abed from previous work and were concerned about his situation, so we decided to work with Joan.

When Joan approached us about removing trees from Abed's field, she suggested we transplant them off the land, as a way to avoid escalating the conflict. Abed agreed.

Action and Arrest

On the evening of May 28, 1996, I and the other members of the CPT-Hebron team—Randy Bond, Bob Naiman, and Tom Malthaner—traveled to the site with Joan and two Palestinians, Faisal and Mahdi, who had offered to be our drivers.

We had just dug up a couple of trees and were preparing to move them when an Israeli military jeep drove by. It stopped and backed up to where we were working. Several soldiers emerged and approached us. They told us what we were doing was forbidden, and they declared the area a closed military zone. This would allow them to take control of the area. Anyone there would be forced to leave or face arrest.

Our team knew, however, that if we left every time soldiers closed a zone, we would never get any work done. Typically, CPTers were given a warning and a chance to leave before being arrested. This had been true in every case during the nearly twelve months I had been in Hebron. But this time it was different. The officers detained us, confiscated our passports, and called Israeli police in Hebron to pick us up. And tragically, Faisal and Mahdi were also detained. Their treatment was likely to be far worse than ours.

From that point on, the situation became increasingly tense. The residents of the settlement quickly discovered that something was up, and a number of them approached us. We were pelted with threats, spit, and stones. Because the Israeli military typically takes a hands-off approach with settlers, the soldiers did little in response.

In her typical fashion, Joan attempted to engage the settlers in "dialogue." She felt it was her mission to reconcile Palestinians and Israeli settlers. This sounds like a good idea, but these two groups were not at a stage where they could dialogue. Dialogue between Israeli leftists and Palestinians might have been possible, or even between right-wing Israeli settlers and peaceniks. But bringing together Palestinians and settlers in Hebron was not.

The more Joan tried to engage the settlers, the more agitated they became. The soldiers, who seemed unprepared to respond to this unusual situation, kept begging us to make Joan stop, which we tried to do. Meanwhile, one young settler was calling on God to destroy us for taking "an angel (the olive tree seedlings) from the ground." At the same time, this man and I engaged in a strange little dance. He kept putting his hand to the side of his mouth as if "hiding" from the soldiers while attempting to spit on me. So I would shift my weight to the opposite side of my body. Then he would switch, and I would switch, until he and I were bouncing back and forth from side to side in a dance of sorts. We both actually smirked.

After four hours, the Israeli police arrived. They loaded us in a police jeep and drove to a police station in the Kiryat Arba settlement on the outskirts of Hebron. There we were kept on a flight of stairs, deprived of sleep, and interrogated for the next fifteen hours. At one point, Bob had a disagreement—the nature of which I don't recall—with one of the officers. Perhaps he had the nerve to ask for a phone call. In any case, the officer responded by shackling the hands and ankles of Faisal and Mahdi, though they had nothing to do with the disagreement. The police then took Bob to a room down the hall, where they sat him in a chair with his back toward us and handcuffed his hands behind him. They left him in this position for more than two hours.

The police continued to refuse us the right to a phone call, though we had been able to contact our lawyer because we had a cell phone with us at the time of arrest. In addition, the police lied to us. They said that if we signed a document and paid a fine, they would release us. CPTers typically do not sign documents written in Hebrew, because we are unable to read them. Joan, Faisal, and Mahdi, however, agreed to the offer. But after they signed the documents, the officers "changed their minds" and would not release them.

Finally, after fifteen hours, the police transferred the men to the military prison of Aduraim, near Dura, West Bank. Joan and I were taken to Lachis Prison in Ashkelon, on the western coast of Israel. I soon found myself in a smelly prison cell wondering what I was supposed to do next.

Waiting in Jail

At the time of my arrest, I had been with CPT's Hebron team for just over a year. I had helped set up the Hebron project and was the team coordinator at the time, having had the most experience of the current team members. I felt competent in this role, but I had just turned twenty-five that month, and on top of everything else, my father was recovering from a heart attack a couple of months earlier, which I had witnessed. I was feeling very emotionally vulnerable. Despite it all, I was stubborn, and the last thing I wanted to do was show weakness in front of the police or the guards. I tried to think about what to do—if there was anything I *could* do.

Our Israeli human-rights lawyer had told us in the past that Israeli criminal prisoners tended to be right wing and that we should talk as little as possible about our work if we were arrested. This was fine with me, but not with Joan. Of the three women with whom we were incarcerated, only one spoke English. (I'll call her Davita.)

It was the eve of Israeli elections for prime minister, and Davita told us she supported right-wing Likud contender Benjamin Netanyahu. Nevertheless, when the women asked us what we were in for, Joan told them the whole story. I had thought being in jail by myself would be bad enough, but I was beginning to think that imprisonment with Joan was worse.

Davita claimed she was in prison for an armed robbery in which she stabbed someone—she was trying to get money for drugs—and that one of our other cellmates was in for murder. Whether or not these were truly their crimes, our cellmates had clearly not kicked their drug habits. Although our cell was immediately facing the front desk, where two guards sat, a fellow prisoner, who apparently had earned special privileges, came by to "visit" now and again. He would open the small metal cover in our door and pass something wrapped in tinfoil to our cellmates. They then proceeded to smoke a white powder off the tinfoil and kept offering the drug to me. Of course I refused. Whatever the drug was, it caused extreme mood swings.

But I figured it was not my mission to convince these women to give up drugs. I thought, "If this is what they need to do to survive in here, I'm not going to bother them." I didn't imagine it would be much fun to kick a drug habit in jail, and I didn't want to make them angrier or more volatile than they already were.

Joan saw it differently, however. Every time the women smoked, she banged on the door and called for the guards. Personally, I figured the guards already knew what was going on in the cell. Every time they came to the window, they had a relatively positive exchange with the women—in Hebrew—and the women went back to their business moments after the guards left.

After a day of Joan banging on the door every time our cellmates smoked, the women were no longer amused. Davita had a knife—a five-inch fruit knife, but menacing nonetheless—and she kept threatening Joan with it. Once, Joan stood relaxed by the door, her elbow resting on one of the bunks, smiling at Davita while Davita hurled curses and threats at Joan, waving the knife at her chest. Joan kept saying, "I know you aren't going to do it," with a benevolent smile on her face. I had to hand it to Joan; she was tougher than she looked—or more naïve.

Davita kept turning to me, yelling at me to get Joan to shut up.

"I have no control over this woman," I would tell her. "She does what she wants."

At night, I tried to sleep while the women muttered to each other. I don't know much Hebrew, but I kept hearing the word *sharmuta*, which means prostitute. It's a very harsh word. The tone in their voices seemed to indicate they were talking about Joan.

I tried to sleep on my bunk, reclining on my belongings so they wouldn't disappear. I worried that the stress of having a daughter in jail three thousand miles away might cause my dad more heart problems.

Troubling Thoughts

And I kept thinking, "How is my being here helping 'the cause'?" Intellectually, I knew there were good reasons to risk arrest when doing nonviolent direct action. Some Christians refer to it as "divine obedience." Many activists—Christian and otherwise—view it as an effective way to draw attention to injustice. Others argue that if you are doing what you believe is right—defending someone from being beaten by soldiers, participating in a public vigil, or standing up for a rightful landowner—arrest may occur "organically" out of the situation. This is the view I tend to hold. But one gets myopic rather quickly sitting in a jail cell, and I struggled to make sense of what I was doing.

Other thoughts occupied me: I had no idea whether CPT headquarters in Chicago even knew we were in jail. Were they feverishly mobilizing the CPT network to deluge the Israeli government with letters on our behalf? Or did they think we were safely tucked in our beds in Hebron? What had we been thinking—sending everyone to assist Abed all at once? The whole team was now in jail. (Standard CPT procedure was to keep at least one person *out* of jail so that CPTer would be available to support those *in* jail.)

But never before had we failed to receive a "leave or get arrested" warning from the police. How spoiled we North Americans are. Palestinians are rarely given warnings. At least I wasn't being tortured—held in a jail cell with lights and music blaring day and night, or held with a smelly black hood over my head, tied in some awful uncomfortable position for hours, or kept in a tiny dark closet where I couldn't stand up straight, or being violently shaken, possibly to death. These are the kinds of things Palestinians face all the time, even after an "administrative" arrest in which no charges are filed.

Joan and I were finally taken to court, and our lawyer didn't show up. We found out later that the police had given her the wrong time. So I was facing a legal system and a language I didn't understand, with no lawyer. But it wasn't all bad: the arresting police officer was nice enough to provide a rough translation.

Joan and I were charged with removing the fence from Abed's land—an action that had taken place weeks prior to our arrest. Fortunately, though, the judge was not playing along. He told the police to come up with something better, something from the night we were arrested. So the next day, the police brought charges regarding the tree removal and numerous other earlier CPT activities, many of which occurred before I was even in the country. This time, the judge was convinced. We had two choices: sign a paper (in Hebrew) agreeing not to return to Hebron until we had left the country and returned on a new visa, or be sent back to jail until our visas expired. For me, this would be three weeks.

I just could not sign the paper.

Joan signed it, and was released. After we returned to the cell, Joan grabbed her things, wished me luck, and was gone. She had left a little present for me, though. Moments later, the guards rushed in; Joan had told them about the drugs again. They made a half-hearted attempt to search the cell. My cellmates merely slipped the drugs under a pillow—hardly a clever hiding place—but the guards still didn't find them. They had a little chat in Hebrew with my cellmates and left.

Soon after that, Davita began pressuring me, telling me I was crazy not to sign the paper. She kept asking what was wrong with me. I tried to explain my decision to her but gave up. Maybe I was an informant, she said, which would explain why I wanted to stay in jail with them. If they thought I was an informant, I would really have a problem. Unbelievably, I was actually missing Joan.

Released—With Conditions

Hours later, my lawyer called, finally getting through to me after trying for days. She was buried in a case involving the Israeli military's expulsion of an entire Bedouin community from their homes in the West Bank in order to make way for an Israeli settlement, yet she was worried about me. "Sign the paper," she advised. "We can appeal later." In retrospect, I think she was overwhelmed with work and was just trying to keep me out of danger. I later learned that an appeal would take forever. I signed the paper and hoped I could turn my attention to getting the other team members out of jail.

The male CPT members had endured their own complicated imprisonment. They were being held in a military camp with Palestinian political prisoners—in other words, people who were likely to be sympathetic to CPT's work. Among the prisoners were Faisal and Mahdi, who kept pressuring the CPTers to "sign the paper, sign the paper." The CPTers sensed that Faisal and Mahdi were being coerced by the guards. Eventually, Bob and Randy signed. After urging from our lawyer, Tom signed a day later, but he was not happy about it.

The four of us went to stay in Bethlehem and decide our next move. Fortunately, a new CPTer, Bruce Yoder, had just arrived in the country. He was able to go to Hebron and tell everyone what was happening with the team. He could also keep an eye on our apartment. Occasionally, he joined us in Bethlehem so we could plan our next step.

After about a week of conferring with our Palestinian and Israeli partners, the CPT office in Chicago, and our contacts in Hebron, the team decided that any member who felt comfortable doing so should return to Hebron. Our contacts explained that the situation there was worsening and our presence was needed. The mayor of Hebron officially "re-invited" us. But we were uncomfortable with having signed a paper agreeing not to return and then returning anyway. So we wrote a letter to the Israeli police in Hebron, stating our intentions:

> As members of the Christian Peacemaker Team who live and work in the Palestinian city of Hebron, we wish to inform the Israeli police that we do not consider our-

selves bound by any order from the Israeli occupation authorities to leave the city.

We consider the Hebron Municipality to be the legitimate political authority in Hebron, democratically elected by the majority of the city's residents and accountable to them. The Hebron Municipality invited us to come to Hebron as a violence-deterring presence because the Israeli police have not protected the Palestinian residents of the city from attacks by Israeli settlers, nor have the Israeli police protected the Palestinian residents from abuses by the Israeli military. . . .

Difficult Decisions

Although I also signed the statement, I decided not to return to Hebron with the others. I struggled with the decision. I told Bob that I felt my stubbornness and pride conflicting with my fear. Bob said there was no embarrassment in not going back. He quoted a line from the 1987 John Sayles film *Matewan*, set in 1920 in the coal mines. One union organizer tells another: "Sometimes you have to bend so you don't break." I thought I might return at a later time, but I was not yet ready right then. I needed to bend for a while.

While my teammates traveled to Hebron, I stayed with friends in the northern West Bank city of Ramallah. It was one of the loneliest times I've had in CPT. I was not proud of myself, even with the bending-versus-breaking rationale. Still, I don't typically make decisions quickly, and I needed to weigh the options.

I began to realize that, on an intellectual level, my decision was to return. But this "intellectual" decision conflicted with my fear of going back to jail.

While in Ramallah, I continued reading the book *Engaging the Powers* by Walter Wink, an excellent study of the historical, religious, and scriptural basis for Christian nonviolence. The book quotes Daniel Berrigan's *No Bars to Manhood*:

> We have assumed the name of peacemakers, but we have been, by and large, unwilling to pay any significant price. . . . [A] whole will and a whole heart and a whole national life bent toward war prevail over the velleities

> of peace. . . . "Of course, let us have peace," we cry,
> "but at the same time . . . let our lives stand intact, let
> us know neither prison nor ill repute nor disruption of
> ties. . . ." There is no peace because there are no peace-
> makers. There are no makers of peace because the mak-
> ing of peace is at least as costly as the making of war—
> at least as exigent, at least as disruptive, at least as liable
> to bring disgrace and prison and death in its wake.[1]

What can I say? I returned to Hebron.

The story does not end there, however. Unsurprisingly, Abed's case remained unresolved. To my knowledge, he didn't person-ally face any consequences from his invitation to us, but his land is still in dispute. The Israeli group Rabbis for Human Rights became involved though, and provided Abed with legal direct-action support, similar to what CPT does.

As for the CPT team, we were not re-arrested, and our return to Hebron led to no immediate repercussions. I went home after spending three uneventful weeks—the time remaining on my visa—in Hebron. A few months later, I was back on a new visa.

Kept Out

One day after returning I was sitting in a park with the CPT team in Hebron's Old City, right across from Ibrahimi Mosque (also called the Tomb of the Patriarchs), where Abraham and Sarah are believed to be buried. A police officer with whom I was familiar approached me. He had been in the Kiryat Arba police station when we were arrested. He was not particularly pleasant.

"I thought you were not allowed coming back to Hebron," he said.

I explained that I had left the country and come back on a new visa, as permitted in the release agreement.

He asked for my passport and took it to a trailer that served as the police station in Hebron's Old City. He photocopied the passport and returned it to me. This did not seem to bode well, but nothing came of it while I was there.

When I left the country, I underwent more than the usual three hours of questioning and a thorough bag search. I barely made the plane.

---

1. Quoted in Walter Wink, *Engaging the Powers* (Minneapolis, MN: Fortress Press, 1992), page 174.

When I attempted to return to Israel a couple of months later, I was denied entry at Ben-Gurion airport in Tel Aviv. The police put me in a holding cell, and a few hours later, drove me to the tarmac where a full plane was awaiting take-off. The police officer handed my passport to the flight attendant and told her not to give it back to me until the plane took off. It made for some interesting stares.

The same thing happened a year later when I tried again to return to the country.

Over the next three or four years, I made some attempts to find out why I'd been kept out of Israel. My U.S. congressional representative even wrote to the Israeli embassy, but they never responded. Finally, while I was working in Washington, D.C., I had a friend with contacts in the State Department. I learned that the Israeli Ministry of Interior wouldn't allow me entry into the country for seven years. They alleged that I had signed a document agreeing that I would not return to Hebron for seven years and that I had violated that agreement. Therefore, I was banned from Israel for seven years. The ban includes the Israeli-occupied West Bank. I tried to find out through my contact at the State Department if the ban was effective from the time of my original arrest date, from the date I was refused entry, or some other date, but I was unable to learn this. Unfortunately, I did not keep a copy of the document I'd signed, which stated I could return to Hebron on a new visa. I doubt that it would have mattered.

I do not regret participating in the tree-clearing action that led to our team's arrest. And I certainly do not regret returning to Hebron. But for a long time I regretted signing that paper. I felt I had "caved" under pressure.

Previous to the arrest in Hebron, I had spent a couple of nights in an Israeli jail. And in an earlier incident, Israeli settlers had attacked CPTer Kathleen Kern and me. But neither situation left me feeling as helpless as this most recent jail experience had. Perhaps it was because I had been cut off from my CPT support. Even though the experience was nothing compared to what Palestinians endure, I sampled the frustration and powerlessness one feels in the face of (seemingly) overwhelming force.

Maybe it was worth it just for that.

CPTers Wendy Lehman (far left) and Anne Montgomery try to intervene on behalf of a Palestinian detainee in Hebron during a demonstartion in Hebron in January 1997.

From the Violence of the Stick to the Violence of the Stomach

Joanne L. Kaufman

Christian Peacemaker Teams' first violence-reduction project began in southern Haiti in 1993, with accompaniment of the community of St. Helene near the city of Jeremie. Members of this parish were threatened by the military dictatorship of General Raoul Cedras. The U.S. military's intervention in 1994 removed Cedras from power. It did not, however, remove other sources of violence from the country.

As the face of violence in Haiti changed, the nature of CPT's work changed. Local partners encouraged CPT to expand its scope from accompaniment in Jeremie to documenting stories of past or present police and legal-system abuses in rural areas of Haiti and, in a larger vision, educating North Americans about their roles in Haiti's "violence of the stomach," a Creole term denoting economic violence.

Accepting this advice, in 1996 and 1997 CPT provided an international presence in rural areas in the Dondon and Grand Anse regions of Haiti and made visits to the Cite Soley slums of Port-au-Prince. Our work centered on giving voice to people with untold stories of violence during military rule under Cedras, a period the Haitians referred to as the "coup" or the "coup d'etat." Inevitably, we also heard about the failures of the current legal system, the fledgling police force, the present Haitian government, and international aid, development, and lending organizations. Despite the removal of Cedras, the hardships were worse than ever.

The conditions under which CPTers worked were physically

and emotionally taxing. Often our listening project seemed far too inadequate. Our local hosts frequently outlined their hopes for economic development projects that were unlikely to be realized by governmental or nongovernmental organizations, whose staffs rarely ventured beyond passable roads. Language limitations and the short time allotted to each visit prevented CPT from following up on the names and dates in the stories we recorded. Nevertheless, CPTers tried to honor the storytellers' sense of outrage, pain, and isolation. This account tracks my reactions and bare-bones notes through several days on assignment in Haiti.

Thursday, November 29, 1996, Pijo

We were tired. Chilly mountain rains the night before had made trails impassable, canceling a dance with which our hosts planned to welcome us. The day began late. CPTer Lena Siegers and I snuggled under the sheets in our generous host's bed, and we bantered with teammates in the next room. Women of the village had been in the cookhouse, crushing and roasting coffee beans, heating water, and pressing cane for our coffee since before dawn.

As we waited for breakfast to be served, we laughed with Brynel, a twenty-six-year-old with sparkling black eyes, a mustache, and a smattering of a goatee on his chin. He was spokesperson for CPT's host organization in northern Haiti, Fondasyon Komite Katye Dondon (FKKD). For the next two weeks, Brynel would lead our team into the hills of northern Haiti to tiny hamlets no white person had visited in decades, if ever. There we would document human-rights violations that had occurred during the Cedras dictatorship, stories of persecution never told to the outside world, or even, according to the tellers, to the Haitian Truth and Justice Commission.

Many FKKD members had been members of the Christian social justice movement, called *ti legliz*—literally, "little church" in Creole. Strongest during the 1980s, this movement emphasized social change and justice for the poor and was fundamental in ending the rule of Baby Doc Duvalier in 1986. Former Catholic priest Jean-Bertrand Aristide, a leader of the *ti legliz* movement, was elected president in 1991 in a landslide. His ousting by Cedras after only nine months in office led to three years of persecution for members of the movement. During those years, beatings were frequent, torture common. Thousands died, were arrested, or abandoned their homes to live in the bush. Thousands also fled to the United States. Many believe that these boatloads of refugees were the primary motivation for the U.S. intervention to oust Cedras in 1994.

That first morning in Pijo, breakfast was coffee and a serving of inch-thick white rolls. Oranges and avocado slices complemented the light meal. After breakfast, Brynel took us to visit the small neighborhood school FKKD had helped organize in Pijo. The school was a pole and coconut-palm-leaf hut, with no desk for the teacher. School structures and paid teachers were hard to find in Haiti. In a rare move, this community had struck out on its own and provided a school for students aged four through twelve. FKKD had encouraged the project with seed money for the structure and blackboards. A local landowner had donated the land for the school. But the teachers and school director had not been paid.

Inside the school, children sat on bamboo poles set in wood forks. Their feet straddled puddles from rain the night before. Brynel brought me to the front of the classroom. The children stopped chanting their lessons and the teacher stepped to the back. In his introduction, Brynel implied that CPT could help find financing for some improvements in the school. He knew better, but he had his own agenda: to get people to trust his organization to find ways to help their projects. I stood in front of seventy-two wide-eyed children who had rarely seen a white person. They assumed that as a white foreigner, I had "lots of money" and would be able to supply some of the school's needs.

I felt tested. How could I deflect what I saw as a kind of begging that undermines self-esteem and belief in the ability to change one's life or government? How could I acknowledge the terrible difficulty of the situation and do it at a child's comprehension level in a language in which I was far from fluent?

I introduced CPT's job as human-rights work and stressed the fact that we could not give aid. I encouraged the children to learn to read and write so they could hold their public officials accountable. "Learn well, so no one takes advantage of you," I told the children.

The teacher and the students' parents all looked as though they were waiting for something. I suspected they would inevitably ask if we could offer aid.

"What concerns you?" I asked. "What kinds of questions do you have for me?"

"We would like a place to sit and write."

"Our feet are eating the mud."

"When the rain comes we run, we fall, we get wet and muddy."

"We need schoolbags."

"My parents can't buy notebooks or books for me."

"The professors cannot buy chalk."

"We have no chairs, no desks."

"We come to school barefoot—it's embarrassing."

"I'm hungry; my parents can't give me food."

"We have no blackboards."

"We want a ball to play soccer."

"We want uniforms for all the children."

"We want a flag to put up when we begin each day."

The litany of need continued when children from the neighboring school trudged up the hill and formed a circle in the muddy yard. By now my teammates had also arrived and had taken over the explanations and listening.

Brynel explained more to me about the FKKD schools project. The organization had helped to start four schools in the outlying regions. "The state only looks at children in town," he said, "children who are

CPTer Joanne "Jake" Kaufman documents stories and images in the Haitian countryside.

'little bourgeois.' We founded this school to help the children of peasants, but we need to find an organization that can help fund these children's education. The schools we started in 1995 cost five dollars (about one U.S. dollar at the time) for each student, but the families don't always pay. So the staff isn't always paid."

When we returned to the school director's drying-clay courtyard, the band was tuning up for the dance that was postponed from the previous night. The pupils in our eyes dilated when we entered the dim house. We saw the singer holding maracas and chanting. A banjo player and two drummers sat on chairs. A bassist held the corner with a one-string bass, masterfully plucking and moving his bandaged digits to create two sounds. An old woman stood next to a cloth-covered table in a back corner of the room, perhaps guarding the *kleren* (sugar-cane alcohol) that sat there.

A steady drumbeat supported the dancers' slow, graceful rhythm. Men and women soon filled the room and the courtyard. Brynel swept me into an awkward dance, as teammate Joshua Yoder took his turn with a little girl. Lena, too, found a willing partner.

Around 11 A.M., the dancing stopped and everyone gathered around a table, at which were seated the secretary and president of the "base," or local FKKD chapter. The secretary introduced Brynel, who stood and delivered a message: "When FKKD came to Pijo, we helped buy blackboards and chalk. But FKKD can't pay the teachers. After nine months, some people have still not paid their school dues. People can't buy enough materials for the school with the five-dollar entry fee, even if it's paid. You must organize if you want schools."

The courtyard became tense. A tall man challenged Brynel. "We don't have money," he said, breathing *kleren* fumes across the table. Any semblance of order quickly dissolved as Brynel discussed the school.

Conducting Interviews

The president of the base rapped on the table. Gaining the attention of some present, he introduced the CPTers as foreigners who had come to record complaints about human-rights violations during the coup d'etat. We quickly decided to split up.

Josh would take notes inside the house, and I would work outside. Lena would talk quietly and informally with the women.

People were still absorbing Brynel's remarks as we tried to get underway with our work. One man with a rough voice and wild red eyes planted his hands firmly on the table where I sat. He peered into my eyes and said, "I can't afford five dollars. I have children to feed. We need a school. I am done."

Sweating now in the sun, I documented the accounts of people more inclined to tell their stories. Some poured out so fast I could not record all the details; others were eked out slowly and painfully but never finished before the next person shoved forward. CPT was unable to track specific dates and times or the identity of the ever-present "they" to whom many people referred. We were limited by the project's schedule, our language skills, and our ability to integrate the information and follow up on it. But "they" can generally be assumed to refer to Haitian military or paramilitary forces.

Below is some of what I heard.

> *Jacksius Orelius.* I was blessed to be able to go to school and become a teacher. In 1984, I entered the *ti legliz* to bring about change. During the coup, they tied me up and beat me. I ran and fell. Father and I slept under the coffee trees. The bugs bit us. We lay down, and something crawled across my feet—a snake. We could not use a flashlight. We escaped because we walked all night.
>
> I was in a demonstration. They took me before the *chef seksyon* (district military commander) and put me in prison. I had to pay for food, and eventually for my liberty. After three years of coup, Aristide returned.

> *Gilbert.* They hit us with batons. I was president of a labor union, but it failed. We need this country liberated! We don't know where to get money. We don't have anything. We don't have enough for a doctor or for medicine. I have three children in school but no mother, no father to help me with them. My daughter had asked for notebooks. I can't give them to her. I can't buy clothes for them to wear to school.

Danius Luc. I have been a militant [that is, an activist] since 1990. I was a teacher in College Prote du Nord in Okap. I couldn't finish my education the normal way because I came out here to hide in the bush. I had a friend who passed me materials to finish. One day I went to Grand Riviere du Nord with my brother. A Sergeant Calos stopped his truck at Carrefour Menard. We were held and they charged us 250 dollars to be freed. Other than that incident, we were in hiding. On September 22, *zenglendos* [bandits] attacked me. I spent 550 dollars at the General Hospital to become well. We demand justice because until today assassins, *zenglendos*, and *macoutes* [paramilitaries] have terrorized us! *Macoutes* in this area continue to terrorize us. We demand justice!

Sylvanie and Helene Cherofin. Women were part of the *ti legliz* too. I was responsible for a small group since 1984. We were on a list. They took me, tied me. I had to pay to be freed. They came behind us. We were in misery.

Though the stories recounted here are a jumble of disjointed phrases in a rough translation of northern Haitian Creole, they convey the villagers' sense of despair and utter abandonment to environmental destruction, political mayhem, and insecurity, and to a cost of living spiraling out of control as hope for meaningful work dwindles.

Finally, no one else came to give an anecdote. We ate a small lunch, then went outside. I started chatting with the people who milled about the courtyard. But the litany of needs and wants began again.

"Can I have your hat?" asked the mother of a beautiful little girl I'd seen earlier in the school. Others also asked for my CPT hat. CPT policy is that only team members may wear the hats. There could be a negative impact if people we didn't know wore the organization's logo around the countryside.

Still, I felt bad for saying no. But these kinds of requests were a game to test foreigners' knowledge of an aspect of Haitian culture: gift-giving is nearly automatic when admiration for something is expressed. But overwhelmed by the stories I had just heard, I shook my head "no" and walked away.

I was coming down with the flu-cold combination that had kept my teammate Pierre Shantz back in Dondon. But something else was bothering me, and I felt weighed down by tears I could not shed. It was about the hat. Even if I could have given away the hat, what would it do? I would be just one more foreigner handing out a manufactured object that would further institutionalize dependency. Part of CPT's purpose in Haiti was to instill a sense of pride and confidence in the fruits of *Haitian* labor—not only in a physical sense but also in an emotional, psychological sense. I almost vomited from weariness with it all.

A Song of Hope in Febros

Minutes later, Lena collected Joshua and me to move on to the next stop, a hamlet called Febros. Brynel had been waiting impatiently for us. It would be a two-hour walk back down the mountain. We hiked the muddy, rocky paths and eventually came to a house with butterflies painted on its whitewashed walls. No one was home but our host's mother. We had missed our meeting.

Dejected, we slouched in the living room and waited for people to arrive again. In time they trickled in, sitting two to a "chair" on sacks of beans, filling the corners of the room.

We joked quietly to raise our spirits. Brynel, suddenly inspired, rose to his feet and began singing in a strong, slightly off-key voice:

> People, people—we are tired of misery,
> If you see me working with my neighbor, it's strength
> I'm seeking!

Everyone began clapping and singing along.

> People, let's assemble;
> Put our heads together to change our country.
> The conch shell is sounding and liberation calls me.
> I'm tired of working to give rich people food.
> I work but I never harvest.
> I plant but they may do what they want.
> We will die or be liberated.

Brynel danced around the room. A drum appeared. The group sang songs from their Catholic Bible-study groups. The vibrant songs lifted our fatigue.

More residents of the hamlet met us behind the house. We clapped our hands with the residents as they gathered. Wild, joyous song rang out. Women wore red scarves on their heads and intricate braids in their hair. Sugar-cane shreds were scattered about on the cement threshing floor, where we sat on rocks and on the sides of chairs made of wood and sisal-coconut fibers. As dark closed in, the serrated leaves of the banana trees seemed to cut the sky into wedges. Insects sang in the background.

Again we heard the stories of people who had been involved in the democracy movement and *ti legliz* (most of the names have been changed.)

> *Berlin François.* Big boots men killed my uncle. They shot him with a gun, in the river. He had a child overseas who sent money to us. The child died of grief.

> *Eobes Robert.* My son's wife was nearing her due date. The police came to arrest him, accusing him of stealing a goat. They came to arrest both man and woman, but he wasn't there. They beat her. They beat him when they found him. Someone paid eighty dollars to the *chef seskyon*, but they kept him anyway.

> *Ti Jean.* No one here slept in their homes. When we left our houses, we put our blankets under our arms. We took to the mountains—three and four of us at a time. We couldn't light matches. We had meetings out there. We each took a child and a mat under our arms. Ants ate our feet. Every night we went to the mountains like that. The women became dry and thin. We didn't have time to make supper. We didn't talk out loud. Each person, in order not to die, paid money to the authorities.

> *Luc.* When I was caught, I took beatings for three hours. My hands were tied behind my back. I was nearly senseless when they finished. The chief told me to stand. I could not, so he kicked me until I defecated and urinated on myself. I had a cow, a pig, and a goat. Nothing

remains. The cow was sold to free me. I spent two months without enough food. We are all in misery and only for the *ti legliz*.

Ketli. We were in the woods, in the mountains. Some people were beaten. Some were not. Women and children stayed in the houses. Cane was all we ate—like rats. People were arrested in Souffriére. All the money in our pockets was taken. People were forced to ask for charity so they could eat.

Jean-Paul. Neighbors slept at our house. *Macoutes* come. I ran, fell, ran. I hid, lay down, and heard the mosquitoes. A nearby charcoal pit popped. I ran, hid, got knocked down. Now I have a bed. I sleep at night. But with justice it is always the same. The court gives no justice. We don't have anything.

Exhaustion

The stories of insecurity, terror, and pain were repeated again and again in the seven or eight villages we visited over three weeks. I was overextended. Our hosts packed our schedule. We used Dondon as a base and walked from village to village, hamlet to hamlet. I was exhausted by the constant movement. The details of everyday living were out of our control: We never knew when we would eat, how clean our clothes would be, where we would sleep, or under what conditions. I'm a shy person and was frustrated by an inability to relate and by a sense that I was "full" of people interactions far sooner than I had expected. I was emotionally and psychologically absorbed by the terrors the Haitian villagers had experienced, but I could do nothing in response. And I felt a sense of accountability—or perhaps guilt—as an American.

These reactions built up inside me until I was barely able to speak to my teammates. At times I was emotionally abusive toward them. Eventually, we were able to work on rebuilding our relationships and our trust in each other.

The morning after our listening sessions in Febros, we walked for six hours back to Dondon. Despite nausea and fever, I kept putting one foot in front of the other, hoping that the virus I was fighting would not completely take hold before we returned to home base. I had skipped a breakfast of greasy plantains and pork sauce, expecting that I probably would have thrown it right back up. Standing at the edge of the last river to cross, I nearly fainted. Our guide carried me across—waterlogged hiking boots and all. I was amazed that Joshua had soldiered through the whole four-day trek despite his difficulties with the same virus.

Many of the stories our CPT team heard in the North had never been documented. Neither the human-rights organizations, nor the Haitian press, nor representatives of the Truth and Justice Commission (charged with documentation and reparations for those who had suffered during the coup) came to the countryside to visit the peasants. They were never compensated for the loss of property, homes, or livelihoods, they said, nor was there much justice for loved ones lost during the coup d'etat.

The people we interviewed across northern Haiti were disillusioned with the government's unresponsiveness to their requests for assistance. Villagers in the remote areas needed agronomists, basic development training, public latrines, public water, roads, schools, and medical care. After our tour of the villages, we wrote: "Many peasants say they will not vote again. One *kazek* (community representative) said he would not run for office again. He said the higher levels of administration are unresponsive. 'I thought I could do something. I had hope in Port-au-Prince to help people, but nothing was ever done. We don't want to do anything with the government again.'"

The peasants have little to show for the taxes they continue to pay. They are afraid to organize or even to meet together. "We suffered so much for democracy, but nothing is happening," said a woman who had been part of the *ti legliz*. The North was once a bastion of organizing for democracy. But after three years, the people of Dondon saw another round of pardons and no compensation or services. Peasants explained how they had been abandoned by the officials they elected to power. "We are the motor of the country, yet we are not being given the gas to function," said one man, pulling up a T-shirt to reveal a washboard chest beneath.

Ears, Hearts, and Voices

On returning to Port-au-Prince, CPTers met with Haitian officials, North American diplomats, and international organizations to talk about the concerns of the peasants. We were keenly aware that we had no funds to offer, no political clout, no aid projects—nothing but our ears, our hearts, and our voices. This felt pitifully inadequate when the need was so great. We had documented the aftermath of violence and terror, but what could we *do*? The work of reconciliation and rebuilding was for Haitians, not for us—as we were reminded again and again by Haitian partners.

But we could repeat what we had learned from interviewing the villagers in the North, and we did at every opportunity in Port-au-Prince. We passed our documentation and notes on to the Truth and Justice Commission, and we spoke with the U.S. and Canadian ambassadors about what we had learned from the Haitians. Later we also bore witness in our North American churches, schools, and meeting rooms to what we had seen and heard.

Some of the peasants voiced the benefits they saw from what CPT was doing. "When foreigners take the time to listen to us," one said, "we gain new self-respect and courage to continue our work." Another added, "You have talents. You are using your talents to listen and understand the violence people suffer here. Now you are responsible to use your talents. Go and tell your people our stories. Have them tell your leaders about the ways they must change so that we can have peace."

The work is not yet over. The witness is not yet complete. My story and the stories of other CPT Haiti alumni will be told again and again. The work of CPT is a continuing story—and a leap of faith. The work of any CPT project can rarely be tied into neat bundles of "accomplished" or "finished." We can never know or absorb the full impact of the stories we have told. We do have hope, though, that our actions and our solidarity bear fruit far beyond our witness.

People of Faith Occupy a Military Base

William Payne

Afternoon prayers: a procession amidst the buildings of the military base, five CPTers, five refugees from the nearby refugee camp, an agitated base commander who's angry that we're in the heart of his base. "Why is it necessary to place his military base next to the refugees?" we ask. The commander, a major in the Mexican army, explains that the military provides social assistance. He comments that the adjacent refugee camp is lacking many basic necessities. It does not even have teachers for the children, he notes.

Abram, an education promoter from the refugee camp, corrects him. "It is true we have no government teachers," he says, "because they did not respect the children or the elders. But of course we have teachers." He goes on to explain to the major that his community doesn't distinguish between the military and the illegal paramilitary death squads. The major accuses CPT of infusing the indigenous people with politics. Ironically, it is they who are politicizing us.

It was nearly Lent 2000. Our CPT team in Chiapas, Mexico, a decidedly pain-filled place, was struggling to find a fitting way to commemorate Christ's Passion. The Christian Peacemaker Teams office in Chicago had provided the Lenten theme: Tent for Lent. The theme was born out of the work of the CPT team in Hebron, where communities are affected by demolition of their homes. How could our team in Chiapas live out that theme? After hours of discussions and meetings with our Chiapas partners, we came up with a plan: We would "occupy" the military base adjacent to X'oyep (Shoy-ep) refugee camp. We would pitch our tent on military property.

Massacre at Acteal

December 22, 1997—this is where I begin my story. Forty-five unarmed civilians, mostly women and children, are cut down in a bloody display of ruthless power. The dead are members of the Abejas, an indigenous, pacifist, Christian group that refused to take sides in the conflict between the Mexican state and the Zapatista rebels. The Abejas of Acteal are devastated and bewildered by the loss. The massacre was perpetrated by paramilitary forces believed to have been armed and trained by the Mexican army, which received substantial aid from the United States.

As a result of the massacre, thousands of Abejas and Zapatistas flee their homes. Like the Zapatistas, the Abejas set up refugee camps within a few kilometers of their villages, and X'oyep is one such camp. Just a few days after the massacre, more than five hundred Abejas walk for several hours on a stormy night to get to X'oyep. The families in the camp, all committed pacifists, welcome the Abejas, feed them, and find dry places for them to sleep. One woman takes seventy people into her two-room house. In the coming days, more Abejas refugees arrive, until more than a thousand people from six different villages have taken refuge there. They stay for nearly four years.

The Abejas was born out of years of struggle against unrelenting violence and injustice. In late 1992, five innocent Mayan men had been charged with murder and jailed by government authorities. Hundreds of people from thirty villages organized prayer vigils, pilgrimages, and demonstrations to demand the release of the prisoners. The villagers committed themselves to nonviolence and chose as their symbol a small, communal stinging insect. The men were eventually released, and the Civil Society of the Bees (the Abejas) was born.

A year later, when many of their neighbors joined the Zapatistas and rose in violent rebellion, the Abejas announced that they agreed with the demands of the uprising, but remained committed to nonviolence. After the 1997 massacre, the Abejas gathered to reevaluate the efficacy of relying solely on nonviolence in their struggle. But even after the horror of the massacre at Acteal, the Abejas chose to recommit themselves to the way of nonviolence.

In the spring of 1998, a few months after the massacre, CPT accepted an invitation from the Catholic diocese in Chiapas to set up a permanent peacemaking team there. A main focus of the team's work would be to accompany the Abejas, which at this time numbered nearly six thousand members, as they struggled to find a just and peaceful solution to the conflict gripping their homeland.

The government had used the massacre as an excuse to send more troops into the region. By the time CPT arrived in Chiapas, there was one soldier for every three civilians in Chenalho, the county where CPT worked. The place was littered with military bases and camps. By Lent 2000, CPT had been in the region for two years and had developed deep relationships with the Abejas. The relationships were forged in the context of a common commitment to the gospel of peace and were based on a willingness to risk life and limb for that commitment. The time was ripe for joint public witness.

During the weeks preceding Lent, our team had several meetings with the leadership of the Abejas to plan a joint Lenten public action of resistance to the militarization of the region. The Abejas rejected our idea of dismantling a military building, preferring an action centered in prayer. We decided to establish a presence on the military base next to the X'oyep refugee camp. The action would be centered on prayer and fasting for the duration of Lent.

The military base had been set up just days after the Acteal massacre. Soldiers had tried to erect the base even closer to the refugee camp than it was now. But they were pushed away by several hundred Abeja women using their bare hands to block the soldiers. Instead, the military set up their "civic action" camp about a kilometer away from X'oyep and hoped to win the hearts and minds of the Abejas with free food and medical services. The Abejas rejected the offer, saying they wanted justice, not handouts from the originators of their suffering.

Setting up the Tent

Fifteen Abejas and six CPTers walk the ten-minute stretch

from the X'oyep refugee camp to the military base and gather
for prayer. We arrive at about 8 A.M., read the Gospel and a passage from Micah, and build the shelter that will house us for
thirty-five days. At noon, we pray. Soldiers visit us, not quite
sure what to make of our presence, and we begin to get
acquainted with them. We erect the "tent" to draw attention to
the fact that thousands of Abejas are living in similar structures
in refugee camps. In reality, a "tent" is a flimsy structure built
of saplings and blue plastic sheeting. We set it up next to the
military flagpole, and the reoccupation begins.

Our press release announces:

> Tent for Lent acknowledges the role of the Mexican
> military in planting the seeds of paramilitary violence
> and fostering division. This campaign of fasting calls on
> us all for a Return: a return of the displaced to their
> homes, a return of the soldiers to their barracks, a return
> to right relationships, and a return in our hearts to a
> centering on God's path of love. . . . Lent is a time to fast
> and reflect, to peer behind the veil of conventional wisdom
> and look at the truth. We are called to proclaim our alle-
> giance to the Kingdom of God, to expose the systems of
> domination that say it is acceptable for the people with
> the most guns to dispossess and exploit the weak.

On the first day of the fast, it is far from certain whether we'll
be permitted to stay on the base. But the military lets us stay.
Perhaps the appearance of the Mexican and international media
has an effect. The military may fear that arresting a group of
foreign "evangelical Christians," as we were called, would bring
too much bad publicity. In any case, the military commanders
do not try to remove us.

We begin a rotating fast, usually involving two CPTers and two
or more Abejas living in the tent. Other team and community
members walk the short distance from X'oyep to the base to
participate in a sometimes grueling cycle of prayer: public cor-
porate prayer every four hours while fasting, night and day.
Sometimes a dozen or more Abejas spend the night in our cramped
tent.

The base itself is simple. Nestled between two hills, beneath a grove of trees, three or four dozen soldiers live in about a dozen humble structures built of local materials. We've built our tent beside the base's soccer field, facing the buildings on the base. Behind us and on the top of a steep hill is the trail the Abejas use to walk to and from X'oyep. A military checkpoint along the trail is manned irregularly by soldiers. At one end of the soccer field, soldiers give out hot meals to the few families who come for them. The Abejas refuse these meals.

We "occupy" the military base adjacent to X'oyep from March 19 to April 22, 2000. It comes to thirty-five days and nights of fasting, praying and discussing.

The Fast

Canadian CPTer Krista Lord and I win the coin toss. We'll be the first to fast for three days. On the first morning of the fast, I wake early to a rustle of activity in the camp. A general from the nearby regional base of Majomut is here, shouting into a field phone, "U.S. . . . Canada . . . *Equipos Cristianos de Accion por la Paz!*" He is a short, stocky man with two graduate degrees from U.S. military universities. He explains to us that the mission of the Mexican military in the area is "social labor."

"Why do the soldiers need guns to provide social services?" Sara asks.

"We are an army," the general replies. "We carry guns."

The general asks many questions about pacifism and the Mennonites, and Sara provides him with a brief history of Anabaptist pacifism. In parting he says, "When you peace people make peace here, we'll leave." We accept his offer.

Pedro, an Abeja catechist, tells the general, "You need to respect the people of this county, Chenalho. Some of you have harmed the people here."

The second morning I wake to sounds of farmers working in an adjacent field and soldiers beginning their day—raising the flag, leaving for town. Ten Abejas displaced from the village of Ybeljoj join the fast, along with two foreign women. Our tent is crowded that night!

Our conversations with the soldiers continue. One day, Alfredo calls me over and asks about fasting. A group of five other soldiers gathers to hear my explanation. I talk about Saint

Francis of Assisi leaving the military and about the Abejas' commitment to nonviolence. We begin discussing the lack of economic options young soldiers are faced with in Mexico, then the major motions for the soldiers to move away from me. But because he is on duty, Alfredo continues talking.

Another day, five men displaced from the village of Yaximel come to join the fast and recount to us the story of how they fled their village the same day as the Acteal massacre. They had also been threatened with violence. The major comes over to talk with us. He argues that the Acteal massacre would not have happened if the military had been present. Sara points out that even with thousands of soldiers in this county, civilians are still fleeing their homes out of fear of paramilitaries. The major replies that the military is unable to intervene on behalf of the villagers. If they took a gun away from a paramilitary, he asserts, there would be ten people with cameras accusing the military of mistreating the peasants.

One afternoon, the county's parish priest, Father Rodrigo, joins us for prayer. "Your presence here makes the military uncomfortable," he says, "and that is a good thing. The indige-

A procession of the Abejas (the Bees) descends into the military base adjacent to the X'oyep refugee camp.

nous have been made to feel uncomfortable in their homes for a very long time. We need to make people uncomfortable with the way things are."

It is a long night dealing with fleas. I guess I need to feel a little uncomfortable too.

In the third week of the fast, members of the original community of X'oyep join us for a day of fasting, including Mariano and Agustin, both more than eighty years old. They are wearing the traditional Tzotzil clothing—a white tunic belted at the waist—and are an impressive sight. I notice that many of the Abejas have gone back to walking right through the base on their way to and from X'oyep, avoiding the arduous trail along the ridge. That night, as I log the day's events, I come across Scott's entry from the previous day: "In an effort to drive us off the military base, soldiers have been playing the Eagles and Whitney Houston. We think we are tougher than that."

As Holy Week approaches, many people, Mexicans and internationals, visit the fast. Many join it for an hour or a day. One day Father Pedro, Sister Josefina, and four other sisters visit and explain that they have been distributing our press release throughout Mexico. Later in the morning we hear the sounds of traditional drums and horns. An Abeja religious procession crosses the ridge above the military base. Many join us for prayer.

During the fast, a new commander is assigned to the base, and he asks to address our group. He talks at great length about how, like the Abejas, he considers himself a pacifist and should not be viewed as a bad person simply because he serves in the military in order to feed his family. He then asks Father Pedro his opinion. Father Pedro's response is respectful but blunt: "Regardless of economics, we must make a choice to follow God's laws and not human laws."

On another occasion, the commander again asks Sara if he may address our group. This time she replies that if he wants to speak with the Abejas, he should ask them himself. It is apparent to us that he's been given instructions to talk with the Abejas while he has the opportunity. Perhaps the military knows, as we do, the value of conversation to bring about conversion. In response to Sara's comments, the commander walks away.

I give a copy of a prayer called "A Litany of Resistance

Against Militarism" to a soldier named Francisco, and later I see him sharing it with several others.

One day a large group of Abejas from Ybeljoj arrives to fast and pray. Later in the morning, the commander sits down with the Abejas, and a man named Vicente decides to talk with him. The major asks Vicente, "Are you a Zapatista?"

"No, an Abeja," replies Vicente, who reminds the major that abejas (bees) have a sting.

The commander tells Vicente that there is already peace here, to which Vicente responds, "I don't see it. What I see are armed soldiers, armed police, and armed paramilitary. I see paramilitary going in and out of this very military camp."

When the major makes an offer of material aid and asks for a meeting at the refugee camp, Vicente replies, "All we want from the soldiers is their departure."

"But the soldiers can't leave until there is peace," the major says.

Vicente challenges him: "There is no peace because of the presence of soldiers and paramilitary, who walk together."

One night during our prayer, I hear a soldier playing with the trigger of his gun. I find this extremely disturbing. It is very dark and we cannot see him, though he is only a couple of meters away. I ask him to stop and am surprised to learn that it's Francisco, with whom I have had many conversations. Maybe he is as nervous as we are.

A new tarp, provided by an Abeja leader, is helping keep people dry during the nightly rains. The nights have gone from hot and sticky to quite damp and chilly, though the Abejas provide plenty of extra blankets to keep people warm. If I position my sleeping mat at just the right angle on the wooden planks, I can sleep for most of the four hours between the two nightly prayer sessions.

Holy Week

The weekend before Easter, a Mexican congressman visits us on his way to the refugee camp. "You CPTers are famous in Mexico," he tells us.

That afternoon Lynn Stoltzfus and I give copies of our "letter to soldiers" to two men on duty. The letters are invitations to leave the military. Later we see the two soldiers reading the letters. It is inspiring to see this small effect of the fast.

On Monday of Holy Week, we hold one of our prayer times on the helicopter pad of the base. Poor Francisco is the soldier on duty, and our presence upsets him. He finally picks up our prayer candle and moves it off the pad.

"That is the light of God," Sara tells him.

"I know," he responds, clearly perturbed, "I'm Catholic."

The Abeja plans for Holy Week include some community actions at the military camp. They plan to hold a community procession through the base on Good Friday, led by a statue of the Virgin of Guadalupe, and on Easter Saturday afternoon they will transform the helicopter pad into a giant peace symbol, a suggestion by the CPTers. We had decided to hold our prayers on the site to get the soldiers used to us going onto the helicopter pad.

CPT director Gene Stoltzfus joins our fast for Holy Week. Many others, including university students from Mexico City and internationals from the United States and Europe, join for short periods of time throughout the week. Our prayer times grow into a powerful anthem, and include several dozen people praying in many languages at once.

Wednesday of Holy Week. Several hundred Abejas enter the military base in a procession behind the Virgin of the Massacre, a statue of Mary that was shot up during the Acteal massacre in 1997. For me it is a highlight of the five-week fast, but the poor soldiers working in the area seem frightened. They run for their buildings at the approach of the procession—a splash of color and spirit, a vision of hope.

Good Friday. The whole CPT team fasts, along with Jose Vasquez, one of the leaders of X'oyep, and his entire family. While soldiers hack at vegetation that has overgrown the razor wire encircling the camp, we form a large prayer circle on the helicopter pad. Our reading is from the Gospel of John: the crucifixion of Jesus.

There is poignant irony in reading about the involvement of soldiers in Jesus's crucifixion as the soldiers surrounding us use machetes to cut away natural vegetation. They reveal cold steel razors while the Abejas reflect on their continued experience of suffering. The prayer is moving.

Holy Saturday. On one side of the base we transform the helicopter pad into a large white "PAZ" (peace) using rocks that were hauled there by the Abejas. We carve into the ground a large sun and moon, symbols of the Creator. On the other side of the camp, the Tent for Lent is dismantled. In its place, flags of peace are raised. The Abejas choir sings songs of freedom in the shade of a nearby tree. More than four hundred participate in this festival of peace.

At the conclusion of the fast, the Abejas present a statement to the Mexican soldiers. In part it reads:

> We announce that we are not against you as human beings. We believe also that you are equal to us, that you are sons and daughters of God our Father and Mother, and of our one Holy Lord who was crucified for our sins. . . . We ask that you listen to our voice and we thank you for allowing us to enter your camp to conduct this action, even as you need to be conscious that you are occupying land which is not yours. This is the land of our ancestors, and your presence with so many arms offends them.
>
> We imagine also that you are capable of conversion . . . and that you have dreams of leaving your military jobs. We believe it is possible that you can return to your barracks so that we can return to our communities of origin. Receive this greeting from the displaced of the X'oyep camp.

Conclusion

What was the fruit of CPT-Mexico's Lent 2000 fast? I admit, it is hard to say. The fast required a great deal of effort, and the results are hard to measure. When we CPTers returned to the military base for our Eucharist on Easter Sunday, we were disheartened to see that the symbols of peace we had created the day before had already been removed. When we asked the commanding officer for the peace flags and banners that had been flying, he immediately returned them to us, neatly folded.

A few months after the fast concluded, I ran into two of the soldiers I had gotten to know during the fast, Alberto and Francisco. Both were thrilled to tell me they had left the military.

Though Francisco had been contemplating leaving the military before we met him, Alberto explained that he left because of our witness.

As I write this, it is more than three years since the fast. Since that time the Abejas have returned to their homes, with CPTers accompanying them on their return journeys. The Zapatistas continue to live in refugee camps. In late 2001, CPT closed its office in Chiapas, though the organization continues to maintain regular communication with the Catholic diocese in San Cristobal and with the Abejas.

Although life has become calm in Chiapas in recent years, violence threatens to return. The fullness of the reign of God remains elusive. We will never know the full impact of our Lenten fast outside X'oyep, but we are called to act in truth and to trust that God is directing the results even when we cannot see them. My hope is that this recollection of our fast in Chiapas will inspire others to believe in the power of fasting and prayer.

As a final word, I offer a few lines from "The Litany of Resistance," which our team recited hundreds of times during the fast:

> From the filth of war, deliver us.
> From the profanity of war, deliver us.
> From the necessity of war, deliver us.
> From the madness of war, deliver us.
> From the blasphemy of war, deliver us.
> From the brutality of war, deliver us.
> From the demonic waste of war and of preparation
>   for war, deliver us.
> Deliver us, O God. Guide our feet in the ways
>   of your peace.

Low-Intensity Warfare and a Girl Named Adela

Tricia Gates Brown

"¡*Buenos dias*!" I chimed, smiling at the young, machine-gun-toting-soldiers manning their post. Tilting my head and waving like the girl-next-door, I could see their steely demeanor melt. "¡*Buenos dias*!" they replied. My heart pounded. Trudging along the path that leads to the Mayan village of X'oyep (Shoy-ep), I almost forgot I was entering a militarized zone. The hills and valleys of highland Mexico luxuriate in jungle green, and the expansive blues of the Chiapas sky lull one's spirit.

I'd come to the state of Chiapas in Mexico with a CPT team to observe the smoldering conflict between the government and the indigenous population of the region. Our delegation had met with Zapatista supporters and nonpartisan nongovernmental organizations (NGOs). We had visited an "autonomous community" where indigenous Mayans live unfettered by the Mexican government, organizing their own health clinics and schools, and building a vital civil society all their own. We'd been introduced to the history of the region. We were nearly experts on the subject of "low-intensity warfare"—a method of warfare in which economic pressure and paramilitary intimidation target the most vulnerable: the young, the weak, the poor, the elderly.

Still, the whole situation was an abstraction . . . that is, until I met Adela. None of it seemed real to me until I got to know this little girl. A couple of days with her were a short-course in "What's Wrong with Low-Intensity Warfare." Adela personified the odd mix of beauty and misery that is the paradox of every Mayan refugee camp.

It was midday when two fellow delegates and I reached the edge of X'oyep. We walked to the center of the village, winding past small refugee shacks with tattered plastic walls and blackened tin roofs. An ornamented Mayan cross in faded turquoise rose at the edge of the dusty village square, our destination.

In the square, a cluster of children stood beaming at us. I approached them playfully and stooped to chat with them in limping Spanish. Immediately, a girl of about eight put her hands to her shoulders and gently pulled her red-bordered prayer shawl over both of our heads, resting her warm, calloused hands on my forearms. The intimacy of the gesture surprised me, but I was buoyant. Under the shade of our tent-for-two, I told the girl my name and learned hers: Adela. We were instant friends.

All the children of X'oyep lavished affection on visitors. Most of them had come there four years earlier, when paramilitary threats drove their families, barefoot and hauling nothing but fear, out of their communities. Paramilitaries—themselves indigenous—supported by the Institutional Revolutionary Party (PRI) had targeted the children's families. The families escaped their villages by trekking miles over muddy jungle trails to communities open to receiving them. The thirteen original families of X'oyep made space for many of these refugees. They shared their beans, corn, and wells with them, and called them neighbors.

When members of my CPT delegation visited X'oyep in July 2001, the population of the village had swelled to more than seven hundred. Water was in short supply and firewood was increasingly scarce. Makeshift shacks for the *desplazados* (displaced persons) stood where cornstalks and beans once flourished. When Adela's family fled her home, she must have been about four years old—old enough to remember.

The children surrounding me held my hands and arms, and stroked my light hair. Their affection was a welcome antidote to the homesickness I felt for my nine-year-old daughter, Madison, who I had not seen for a week and to whom I am doggedly attached. In the few days before I left, she'd been distraught. She had sobbed herself to sleep at night, clutching me and begging me not to go.

The village square also served as the children's playground. They would amble down to the square throughout the day to jump rope, to play tug-of-war with the one rope they shared, or to rally their international *compañeros* for a game of duck-duck-goose. I sat in a sliver of shade alongside the simple, wooden guesthouse, mesmerized by the children's ability to spin a game out of thin air. The girls were a rainbow of brightly woven shirts. They each donned the embroidered patterns distinctive to their home communities, while the boys wore threadbare T-shirts displaying the likes of Mickey Mouse or Jean-Claude Van Damme.

When I pulled origami paper out of my backpack to fashion peace cranes for the few children around me, I was rapidly swarmed. The children pressed in so close I could smell their sweat and the dust that had settled on them like dew. I could feel their hot breath. As I busily creased the paper into intricate folds, they taught me words in Spanish and in their Mayan language, Tzotzil. I took out the picture I'd brought of Madison, and the children studied it carefully, gawking at the photo in which Madison wore glasses and was crouched beside a kangaroo in captivity. By the time the last child sat patiently beside me, elbow pitched on my lap, I'd made a flock of twenty cranes.

Abejas girls play in the open-air chapel of the X'oyep refugee camp.

The following morning, the open-air chapel beside the square stirred like an anthill. In one half, men gathered for a meeting; in the other, women and girls sat down on doll-sized wooden chairs to begin their embroidery. Seeing an empty stool next to Adela and her mother, I approached them and took a seat. Adela's mother had gentle, knowing, coal-black eyes, a bewitching smile, and dense, dark hair that fell to her waist. She was lovely. The edges of her eyes and mouth bore the lines of sun and weather, making her appear older than my thirty-one years, though I later learned she was only twenty-seven. Like the other Mayan women, she was petite, and I marveled at the size of her plastic shoes. We talked about stitching and about our children. I learned Adela had two younger siblings. Adela's mother stitched with brightly colored yarns spooling out of plastic bags on the dirt, but managed to keep her cloth a gleaming white. The women's conversation punctuated the morning with levitating tones, and I could not stop smiling.

At intervals throughout the morning, a man at the front of the chapel would call people to prayer, sing-songing the announcement in a characteristic Tzotzil manner. All the men and women would kneel on the gravelly, dirt floor of the chapel and commence to pray. They prayed this way for five minutes, every hour on the hour. My knees ached. The style of prayer involved everyone simultaneously lifting up individual vocalized prayers, and the cacophony of whispering voices at first swelled around me like a fearsome undertow. It called to mind the disquiet of the charismatic prayer meetings I'd attended as a child.

Then something in me shifted. The voices began to rise to the pitch of a resonant choir, and I was lifted up by them. I heard the women's voices most distinctively. Their prayers sounded urgent. They were praying for the safety and future of their children, I guessed, and I begged God to answer them. My thoughts wandered to my own daughter, as sheltered from danger and need as a captive kangaroo.

During one of the breaks between prayers, Adela kept asking if I would like to buy a purse she had embroidered. At first I couldn't make out her words. There was no sound. Just her lips exaggeratedly mouthing the question: "*Quiere comprar una bolsa?*" Do you want to buy a purse? For some reason, she made the words inaudible. When I finally cracked the code I said, "No, thank you," then immediately regretted it. I had bought a purse from a girl in the last village, and buying two seemed excessive. But it dawned on me—woefully late—how hard it had been for Adela to ask.

After a while, I awkwardly told her I wanted to buy one of her purses, and her face lit up. With her mother she led me— weaving between the refugee shacks, stepping over wastewater ditches, ducking under sagging clotheslines—to a wood-sided building at the back of the camp. I bought the purse, wondering why their house had wood siding and was larger than the others. Then we returned to the chapel, shortly before prayers disbanded.

We CPTers, along with two other visiting internationals, ate three times a day in a kitchen measuring eight by ten feet. Smoke billowed through the roof from the open fire, where tortillas were baked throughout the day, and beans bubbled in large blackened pots. In the middle of our lunch the skies opened to a jungle downpour. Sheets of water made rivulets along the dirt paths and transformed ditches into rivers. From the kitchen, I noticed Adela and two friends crouched under the eaves of the *compañero* house. I quickly mopped up the last of my beans with a warm tortilla and ran to invite them into the guesthouse for shelter.

We waited out the rain on the end of the bed next to our door, watching the sky fall before us. We talked and laughed, and I sang them songs: "This Little Light of Mine," "We are Marching in the Light of God," and "Do-Re-Mi." Adela returned the favor, singing a song to me. She then began to teach me the Tzotzil numbers, situating her face about two inches from mine, forever etching on my memory the look of her full lips, enunciating the edgy syllables of the Tzotzil numerals, and the deep well of her giggle. She asked to see the photo of my daughter again, and I pointed to Madison, saying, "She is your friend." Adela replied, "Yes, she is my friend." I basked in our wide circle of friendship: Madison, Adela, and me.

In Chiapas, CPT worked closely with the indigenous pacifist Christian group *las Abejas*—which means "the Bees"—from 1996 to the end of 2001. The Abejas are a highly organized society who support the struggle for indigenous rights in Mexico —the rights to live and work communally as the Maya have done for hundreds of years—but do not support the taking up of arms. According to the Abejas, violence is incompatible with faithfulness to Jesus, who calls his followers to love their enemies. "As bees have only one queen," they explain, "we have just one Lord." As they see it, they cannot serve Jesus and kill their opponents.

These convictions render them especially threatening to paramilitaries in the region and particularly vulnerable to violence. In December 1997, in a nearby village called Acteal, forty-five Abejas men, women, and children were murdered by paramilitaries in a massacre that went on for eight hours. After this massacre, Christian Peacemaker Teams and other international peace groups stepped up their accompaniment of the Abejas.

Something about the Abejas broke my heart—in both the best and the worst senses of the phrase. In their tireless generosity, in their ardent desire to see the redemption of their enemies, in their joy, in their meekness, in their self-sacrificing and uniting love, they model what it means to be a follower of Jesus. Observing these qualities in them melted my chronic cynicism. I saw among them a faith so real it inspires hope and an active love that breathes life into jaded onlookers—whether they are overchurched Western Christians or skeptics of religion. I saw both types weep on hearing their story.

But it also broke my heart to realize they are an endangered people—not only the Abejas, but all the indigenous people of the Chiapas region. The Maya have the odd misfortune of living in an area rich with natural resources and biodiversity. Corporations are just waiting to turn those resources into profits, and many in Mexico and the United States are eager to see the Chiapas highlands exploited. At best, the indigenous population is viewed as a source of cheap labor; at worst, as impediments and troublemakers. The governments of Mexico and the United States are so committed to the path of "liberalized" trade, that dissent has no place in their lexicon. President George W. Bush, with his Free Trade Area of the Americas (FTAA), and Mexican Presidente Vincente Fox, with his Plan Puebla to Panama (PPP), envision a future for southern Mexico much different from the one most Maya would choose. The indigenous live on land they have populated since the Spanish conquests, and they are in the way.

On the morning of my third day in X'oyep, I planned to leave after breakfast. I ate quickly, hoping to have time to tell Adela good-bye. I meandered back through the squalid area where the displaced families were at their household chores, to the wooden building where I'd bought the purse. No one answered my knock, and a woman in a nearby shack told me no one was around. I turned and walked back to the guesthouse, struggling against mounting tears. The tears took me by surprise. I had not planned to feel such loss at leaving this village, where I'd spent only two nights and less than two full days.

I wrote Adela a short note of farewell, carried it to the woman at the shack and asked her to deliver it. When I had nearly reached the bottom of the hill again, I heard someone call "Teresa," the name I'd adopted in X'oyep. It was Adela and her little brother, Samuel, who were laughing as they ran down the hill.

The three of us sat together, talking only a little. Adela explained that her parents had gone to a nearby village to work for the day. I suspected they worked as contract day laborers. Since NAFTA (the North American Free Trade Agreement), many Mexican farmers, put out of the farming business by foreign, subsidized corn, have been forced to survive in this way. Adela and Samuel leaned on my lap and held my hands, and I looked away so they would not see the wetness of my eyes. After a few minutes, Adela asked me to show her the photo of Madison again. When I found it, I wrote on the back, "Madison, the daughter of Teresa," in Spanish, and gave it to Adela.

Adela invited me to her house to meet her grandmother. I was led by skipping children on the end of each of my arms. When we arrived, however, we were not at the building I had seen the previous day, the one with the wood siding and the padlock on the door. It dawned on me—again more slowly than it should have—that yesterday we had been at the women's *workshop*.

The place where Adela actually lived was a tiny, feeble-looking frame covered in blackened plastic sheeting that was torn in many places. Inside the structure were household items—a couple of pots and plastic bowls, a few plastic sacks heavy with their contents—and little else.

Adela offered me a diminutive wooden chair, one of three scattered around the floor. Though her grandmother was not home, her aunt sat near the door, stitching in the light of its opening. We took seats next to her. I bounced Samuel on my lap, chanting to him a silly English rhyme, as Adela picked up her embroidery and continued stitching a perfect blue pattern onto the dusty white linen.

I knew my teammates were ready to leave and I could not stay long. I tried to tell the children I did not want to go, but my inept Spanish seemed especially inadequate to express the subtleties of good-bye. I gave the children hugs and left X'oyep.

Less than two weeks after I visited the village, the Abejas announced that most of the displaced communities in X'oyep would be returning home. Among them would be the community of Adela and her family. The scarcity of resources in X'oyep had, in part, forced these communities to make the difficult choice: they would face the presence of paramilitaries back in their villages rather than further deplete the resources of X'oyep.

A friend of mine later returned to X'oyep with CPT to accompany the refugees back to their homes and to reside in their villages for a time. He delivered an envelope to Adela for me. It contained a drawing, a letter, and a photograph of me with Madison.

The Abejas families who returned home from X'oyep reintegrated into their communities successfully, inspiring Abejas families from other communities to leave their camps and go home. In a massive Abejas homecoming late in 2001, CPT accompanied the returning families and monitored conditions in their villages. A few stories emerged of former paramilitaries reconciling with their Abejas neighbors upon their return. For the most part, however, relations between them remain tense.

The struggle for indigenous rights in Mexico continues. The outright violence of paramilitaries has given way to more subtle forms, such as economic oppression and constant military intimidation. The government of Mexico has failed to make good on its promises to the indigenous population and continues to pursue a neoliberal economic program for Chiapas, contrary to the demands of the indigenous movement. Low-intensity warfare persists.

I wonder what Adela's life will be like when she is my age. Will she and her husband farm like her ancestors of countless generations, or will she work in a sweatshop where pregnancy tests are compulsory and where she breathes carcinogenic air? Will she wake each morning to the unadulterated natural grandeur surrounding her village, or will the monochromatic gloom of urban poverty encompass her? Will her family's life be punctuated by the rhythms and seasons of Mayan tradition, or will advertising and technology shape the desires and lifestyle of her children?

The Abejas teach us many things about sharing, cooperative work, care of the land, commitment to community, peacemaking, and hospitality.

Adela, I wish you more of these.

Dispatches from the Front

Father Bob Holmes, CSB

(For their protection, most names of Colombian civilians, guerrillas, and paramilitaries have been changed.)

January 18, 2002

Though I expected to be in Hebron come January, I find myself in Barrancabermeja, Colombia. With CPT's blessing, I joined the team here.

Barranca is situated on the Magdalena River, in the north-central region of Colombia, though our peacemaking work is mostly on a tributary, the Opón River. Barranca is not a nice place. It's an industrial city around an oil refinery. And it's hot!

My orientation to this very violent place has had a steep learning curve, and perhaps the best way to introduce the many players in the drama is to take you through my first days here.

Our CPT house in Barranca is in an area that was under guerrilla control until October 2000. At that time, the United Self-Defense Forces of Colombia (AUC) paramilitaries took over, eliminating anyone with real or imagined connections to the guerrillas: ninety-eight people were killed in our *barrio* (neighborhood) in 2001 alone. On my first evening in Barranca, we visited refugees from the Opón. They were sheltered in an old, unused teachers' college. They are the farmers and fishers we are accompanying home. Thirty-three families have already gone back, and thirty-seven more hope to return soon.

I heard stories of harassment, disappearance, and assassination suffered at the hands of the paramilitary. The injustices have caused the flight of whole communities to Barranca. The families dare not return unless we go with them—and stay with them.

My introduction to the paramilitary came on a visit to a barrio near the river. As we walked along, several young men hailed team member William Payne by name. They recognized him because of encounters he'd had at a paramilitary checkpoint upriver, where he'd been "getting in the way."

It was time for my first trip to the Opón, using CPT's motorized steel canoe. Regular drivers are supplied by the communities we accompany. At the checkpoint on the Opón stood four armed paras (paramilitaries). They were not in uniform, and each carried a handgun or a small automatic weapon. We stopped, and teammate Matt Schaaf went ashore to talk and pray with them. We try as often as possible to engage the armed men and women in prayer for peace and an end to violence. They usually respond with at least a quiet tolerance. I remained in the canoe, protecting the driver. That night we stayed in the driver's village.

In the morning, we rode an hour and a half further upriver to the railroad bridge, where we met CPTers William, Lisa Martens, and Lena Siegers. They had come by railroad on a small cart pushed along by a motorcycle—the Motorola. The team continued upriver to a para-controlled town, hoping to meet with a local para commander. He wasn't there, so we prayed with a group of those living in the town, using the biblical passage about Saul's conversion from violence to nonviolence on the road to Damascus. Afterward, Matt and I went downriver while the other team members found land transport back to Barranca.

The next day we followed a long, narrow channel to Ciénaga Lake, so I could be oriented to the location of the next refugee return. The abandoned village was overrun by wasps, especially the school, which was also covered with paramilitary graffiti.

I piloted the ten-meter-long canoe back out of the twisting

channel. At the checkpoint, Matt played peace and justice songs on his guitar for the paras—one more way to sow seeds of nonviolence in the minds and hearts of people carrying guns.

After four nights in the *campo* (countryside), it was time to return to the city. Along the way, a family warned us of heavy gunfire downriver. As we got closer to the checkpoint, we were told that FARC (Revolutionary Armed Forces of Colombia) guerrillas had fired on paramilitaries in their canoe, wounding and possibly killing some. At the checkpoint we observed fresh FARC graffiti.

It was known that FARC was in the area, but lately the guerrillas had been keeping out of sight. The people of the Opón had suffered violence in the past, but not recently. This latest incident could lead to retaliation against the civilians, to discourage collaboration with the guerrillas. In the city, the team heard from paras that three of their comrades had been wounded in the shooting, but none had been killed. At our team meeting, we decided to speak out against violence on all sides of the conflict, calling for nonviolent ways of resolving disputes. We issued a public statement denouncing the killings and distributed it widely.

January 18, 2002

Because of its violent acts against civilians, the AUC paramilitary has been identified by the United States as a terrorist organization. The Colombian army and navy deny any connection to this outlaw group, which operates openly in the Opón, the area where CPT provides accompaniment for the civilian population. Last week, our team saw men known to us as AUC members together with navy personnel at the usual AUC checkpoint on the Opón.

A few days later, CPT led a delegation of Colombians from Barranca to the Opón and stopped at the same checkpoint, not occupied by AUC at the time (we had warned them we were coming). We offered a prayer—an "exorcism" of sorts—calling on God to drive away the evil spirits of violence, intimidation,

CPTer Lisa Martens burns a "death list" with Colombian villagers from the Opón River area, where CPT provides accompaniment.

and fear, and to replace them with the holy spirits of nonviolence, justice, and peace. The delegates, mostly human-rights workers, then proceeded upriver, stopping at villages along the way to hear the stories of the people. At the last stop they were fed fish and yucca, eaten off banana leaves. The day before, teammate Carol Foltz Spring and I had helped prepare the site for the meal, and because I was the only one not barefoot, I was appointed to crush with my heel the four scorpions we exposed as we lifted boards off the ground.

One village on the Opón remains empty, its former inhabitants still living as refugees in Barranca. They plan to return home soon, with our accompaniment. Last Thursday, four CPTers approached the village to check it out and saw smoke and flames. They found about two dozen armed AUC members "clearing" the land, which included burning five or six houses to the ground. The arrival of the team probably saved other houses from being destroyed. The paramilitaries seek to extend their control through intimidation and fear; we seek to stand with those suffering as a result of this oppression and to reduce violence by being present.

February 5, 2002

Violence reduction is what CPT is about. Along the Opón River, this entails accompanying people threatened by both legal and illegal armed groups. The civilians we accompany are caught between guerrillas and paras, threatened by both groups for supposed collaboration with "the enemy." To be proactive, we seek to engage each of the armed groups in dialogue.

Last week, teammates Scott Kerr, Lena, and I journeyed deep into guerrilla-held territory. There we talked with Juan, the regional guerrilla commander. We had three hours of intense discussion.

Asked about his vision for the future of Colombia, Juan replied, "A time of justice for all—economic, political, and social justice in which all people can live with dignity." When we challenged his idea that the end is in the means, that a peace achieved through violence can only be maintained by threat of violence, he launched into a history lesson. Fifty years ago, he explained, the left was politically organized but suffered a massive wave of assassinations, forcing them into armed rebellion. We reminded him that the past fifty years of violence had not produced peace, and we encouraged him to think in new ways. He asserted that as long as the United States continued to support his enemies, a just peace was not imminent.

CPT had publicly denounced the guerrilla attack on paramilitaries that took place on the Opón the week before. We gave Juan a copy of the denouncement. He had already read it. He told us that, while he respects our role and will not hinder our work, if the enemy is in our area, the guerrillas will be there too.

This week we entered para-held territory, but the circumstances were quite unique. For the first time in years, people from the villages whom we accompany on the Opón traveled upriver to this territory to play soccer against a local team. CPTers accompanied the team and its supporters: forty-six people in three overloaded motorized canoes. It was "Superbowl Sunday," and unfortunately, the visitors lost. But barriers were broken and old friendships renewed. Food, drink, and music followed the game, and it was a joy to watch the children mix and dance together.

As the celebration wound down, some uninvited guests arrived: a dozen armed, uniformed paramilitaries. A public accusation of collaboration with the guerrillas was followed by tense discussion; downriver folk moved anxiously to their boats. It was good that we were there.

Arriving home in the evening, we found several human-rights workers with leaders of the displaced community we accompany in Barranca. They were terribly upset and told us that one of the community members had been abducted by paras while walking on the streets. He was the leader of the civilians that we accompany. What to do?

Despite the late hour, Pierre Shantz, Lisa, and Jim Fitz immediately headed to a para-controlled neighborhood and spoke to a local para leader, who denied any knowledge of the kidnapping. The next morning, Jim and I took part in a meeting of all the human-rights groups at the refugee center where the displaced live. There we helped write a public denouncement of the abduction. The abducted man is still missing, despite rumors of his death or that release is imminent.

February 17, 2003

For a change and a rest, I traveled to the beautiful city of Medellin, seven hours away from Barranca by bus, to stay with my Basilian brothers there (I am a member of the Basilians, a Catholic religious order). I discovered that their *barrio*, to which my taxi driver was very reluctant to take me, suffers from the same war as the *campesino* area where CPT works. There were thirty-eight violent deaths there in 2001. Still, my time there was a blessing—talking with old friends, reading, enjoying cool nights—even a bullfight, my first and last!

Arriving back in Barranca I found the team caught up in three new crises. The day before, someone (likely paras who control the port area) had laced our gasoline with salt. The boat motor would have been destroyed if it were turned on, but the hurried, sloppy vandalism job left noticeable traces of salt in the bottom of the boat. Then, on the Opón River, guerrillas had tied up and threatened two fishermen, who were released only when the guerrillas heard a boat approaching. Perhaps they thought it might be CPT. Also, the Colombian army, making an incursion into the guerrilla-held Cimitara Valley (another area where CPT sometimes accompanies civilians), had used our boat and flown the CPT flag to cross the river and look for guerrillas. We never allow armed persons in the vehicles we use, and we denounced each of these violations publicly.

The next day I joined Scott in the Cimitara Valley. As we traveled the river we noticed that, with the army in the area, the guerrillas had melted away into the forest, and many civilians had fled their homes. We were repeatedly told that CPT's presence was a strong deterrent to army violence against civilians suspected of collaboration with guerrillas.

We were asked to accompany two female development workers to a meeting of a sugar cooperative. The trip would be two hours upriver by boat and six hours into the mountains by horse. Three of those hours would be in the dark. But I learned from my first time on a horse that they can see in the dark, even if I can't. Some unexpected ups and downs made for an exciting ride.

At the meeting, we heard stories of paramilitaries threatening lives and stopping food and medicine from entering the area. On the return journey, we noted a guerrilla presence along the way, a sure indication that the army incursion was over.

When we returned to Barranca, we learned of the success of a CPT Ash Wednesday action at the paramilitary checkpoint on the Opón. CPTers had occupied the checkpoint, hung beautiful prayer banners made by the river communities, set up our tent, and invited the communities to the celebration. The paras didn't join the forty-or-so celebrants. A meal was shared, and the Lenten season began with prayers and the burning of a death list. The ashes of the list were mixed with the ashes of homes burned by paras. And we read the following liturgy:

Up From the Ashes: A Liturgy
Welcome: Today we call to mind those listed for death in
Colombia and around the world, and symbolically burn the
death lists. Then we pray insistently for new life to rise up
from the ashes.

Leader: O Creator, Source of our peace,
         From the shadow of death over Colombia,
         from the death lists of the armed groups,
         from intimidation and fear,

People: Deliver your children.

Leader: From our complicity in the killing,
         From profiting by arms sales,
         From providing training for those who kill

People: Deliver your children.

Leader: From the violence of war everywhere,
         From enlisting of youth in armed groups,
         From the suffering of innocent victims,

People: Deliver your children.

*(Burning of a death list while praying silently for a cleansing
regeneration of hearts and minds.)*

Leader: By infusing hope in the midst of death,
         By transforming the hearts of those bearing arms,
         By enlightening armed leaders in the power of non-
            violence,

People: Raise us up from these ashes.

Leader: By our rejection of violence as a means to justice,
         By our refusal to cooperate in the export of violence,
         By our confronting of unjust systems,

People: Raise us up from these ashes.

Leader: By seeing your image even in enemies,
         By teaching all children to celebrate life,
         By converting economies of greed to ones of sharing,

People: *Raise us up from these ashes.*

All: *O Loving Creator, grant us peace. Amen.*

Big War, Small War, Dirty War

The peace negotiations have broken down between the Colombian government and the FARC guerrillas, bringing all-out war to areas far south of us. That's the Big War covered by the international news. So far, we are untouched by the Big War.

The Small War is going on here. Sometimes the Colombian army makes incursions into guerrilla-held territory, where we accompany civilians. The guerrillas fade into the countryside and the army accuses civilians of collaborating with the FARC. Many families flee until the army leaves. Sometimes during these incursions, the guerrillas hit and run. They sneak up on the army, fire a few shots, and quickly disappear. This too endangers the civilians as the army responds indiscriminately with heavy gunfire and grenades.

But it is the Dirty War that is most frightening. It targets civilians. It is waged with threats and death lists, abductions and assassinations, massacres and displacements. The guerrillas have done all these things at one time or another, but it is the paramilitaries' preferred mode of operation. Illegal and unaccountable to any authority, the paras act as vigilantes, taking the law into their own hands. Their target is not the elusive guerrillas, but the guerrillas' clandestine support networks and suspected sympathizers among the civilian population. Community leaders are high on the paras' lists. It's called "drying up the water where the fish swim"—a method taught to Latin American military officers at the School of the Americas (SOA) at Fort Benning, Georgia. This technique was used with terrorizing effectiveness in counter-insurgency wars in El Salvador, Guatemala, and Chiapas, Mexico.

Many of the families we accompany on the Opón River have lost fathers, sons, and brothers to the paras. In the past two years, whole communities have fled their river homes in fear. In May 2001, they began returning with CPT accompaniment. Last October, the fifteen-year-old son of one Opón family was abducted and murdered by paras in the port of Barranca. Just last week, paras walked into villages we accompany. CPT talked with the paras and stayed close behind as they moved on. Coming to the para-operated checkpoint at the mouth of the Opón is always a fearful moment for the *campesinos,* who never know whose name might be on the list. CPT tries to be present as much as possible.

Our Lenten action is to pray each week at a place of violence. On Ash Wednesday, at the para checkpoint, we read a death list, burned it, and prayed for new life. The following week we did the same in the port area of Barranca and planted a tree in the ashes. Last week we traveled to the village of San Francisco in the Cimitara Valley and repeated our liturgy.

It was a hot, dusty trail on which Lena, Scott, and I set out in the Ciénaga area. We were following up on a rumor of violence in the small, eight-family village of La Reforma, not far from the Opón River, where we accompany families living under constant threat. A young boy on horseback was our guide until he turned off, saying, "Go that way."

We learned that on Tuesday, March 5, the paramilitaries had come to La Reforma and abducted Pedro Vegas, who had no family in the area, as he returned from working in the fields. He was taken along a trail and shot dead. We prayed at the blood-stained site. Was this farmer a guerrilla in disguise? Was he a civilian supporter of the guerrillas? Did he have a brother or sister in the guerrillas? Or was his murder a random one calculated to intimidate the families in the area? No one knew or would say, but there was no doubt about the fear engendered. It was palpable.

La Reforma is near the abandoned village of Ciénaga. Those who lived there are now refugees in Barranca. A month ago Manuel Navarro, a leader of this displaced community, was abducted in the city port. He is believed dead. CPT is committed to accompanying the community's return, but with Manuel disappeared and another leader forced to flee for his life two weeks ago, the community has postponed their return. The murder of Pedro reinforces their fear.

It's a dirty, stinking war—Pedro and the families of La Reforma among its latest victims.

By 10:30 A.M. we had documented the assassination and prayed at the site. The Motorola wasn't returning to Barranca until 5 P.M., so we decided to walk to Ciénaga Lake—an hour further, according to the folks in La Reforma. It was noon when we got there, soaked with sweat and almost out of water. *Ciénaga* is Spanish for swamp and we had no inclination to put the swampy water in our water bottles. Nor had we brought food. On the way back, after walking an hour in the blistering sun, we accepted swampy water from a farmer (he drank it, so why couldn't we?). Shortly after drinking it, I threw up. The next two hours were hell. Dehydrated, desalinated, dangerously low on carbohydrates, muscles cramping, and head dizzied, I barely managed to make it back to the railroad. Alas, we had vastly underestimated the challenge.

Basta! Enough! Too much! Even one death is too many!

It is not just the *campesinos* in places like La Reforma who have to deal with the paras. Paramilitaries are actively establishing control in the city too. There is a huge oil refinery in Barranca, and the workers are very organized. Three union leaders have been assassinated by paramilitaries in the last three months here. The third organizer was killed just last week, and CPT became involved in the funeral.

CPTers Chris Schweitzer, John Marks (an intern), Pierre, and I attended the wake at the Union Hall for Rafael Jaimes Torra, treasurer of the Federation of Labour Unions (USO) of Barrancabermeja. He had been gunned down in front of his home as he got into his pickup truck on the morning of Wednesday, March 6.

Friday had been the day for our weekly Lenten action, and because the wake was on a Friday, we asked the union members if they would welcome our prayerful witness of publicly burning a death list in places threatened by armed violence and assassinations.

"Absolutely!" they responded. "We welcome your support."

Several hundred mourners gathered in the street as Pierre invited them to join us. In prayerful litany we asked our Creator to free us from the shadow of death cast by the many armed groups in Colombia. Then Chris laid out a page of chart paper and people were invited to create a symbolic "death list." Name after name was written down of persons known to be targeted by one or the other armed group—so many that a second page was needed. My eyes, and those of many others, were filled with tears as we reflected on the names being inscribed. There was eerie silence as Chris burned the list.

Again, in litany, we begged God to lift us up from the ashes with new hearts, new hope, and new light. John poured the ashes into the earth, and he and I planted a young tree in the pile. With the body of Rafael Jaimes a few meters away, I think we all knew that only by God's power could the tree of life rise up from the ashes here and throughout Colombia.

It's Good Friday. In Barrancabermeja, Colombia, across the street from the mayor's office, CPT is bearing public witness to the violence of legal and illegal armed groups. They all have death lists.

> A death list read—Jesus is condemned.
> Bodies on the ground—Jesus dies.

Colombian Mennonites and Catholics from Bogotá have joined the CPT team for Holy Week and are participating in this heart-rending tableau. In the search for a just peace, we are calling out to all the world for an end to the violence.

> The death list is burned, the ashes poured into the earth—Jesus is buried.
> A tree is planted, the bodies lifted up—there is hope of new life.

It's Easter morning, and again Colombians rise with the team and help lift a seven-meter-high banner naming all those whose lives need to be honored and protected.

A Life List is raised high—Jesus lives.
The fast is broken—Jesus's disciples sent.

The Colombians return to Bogotá with renewed passion and determination to labor for a just peace. The team heads upriver to continue the accompaniment of fisher families living under constant threat from armed groups.

There is hope of new life in Colombia.

Singing Through Our Fears

Carol Foltz Spring

"Why are you afraid? Have you still no faith?" (Mark 4:40)

I always took for granted the safety of my own bed at night, and I have been blessed once again to return home to "safe" places (though many Americans now feel less safe than they used to). But I remember a friend in Colombia who has two babies at home. He lies awake at night listening for the slightest noise— a snap of sticks underfoot or a rustling of leaves. When morning comes, he is exhausted. What choice does he have? He cannot leave his small farm, his family, his community.

The war in Colombia is not primarily about bullets and tanks and killing "the enemy," but about controlling the civilian population through carefully planned fear campaigns. Every group that carries weapons—guerrilla, paramilitary, army, navy, or air force—seeks control over the forty million civilians, and the psychology of fear plays a big part in that control.

I had been in Colombia for one week, having spent the first few days in Bogotá for orientation with the Mennonite Church of Colombia before I joined my CPT mates at the beginning of Holy Week 2002. I went immediately to the countryside with teammate Scott Kerr, riding two hours on bumpy dirt roads to the region of the Cimitara River Valley. On the return trip several days later, we decided to ride on public transportation, which meant we'd ride in a decrepit truck outfitted with a pair of narrow benches and wooden slats to keep people and goods from falling out the back. We wanted to accompany the people in what can be a fearful journey—crossing from guerrilla-controlled territory to paramilitary-controlled territory. It's a journey they must undertake for the simple task of going grocery shopping.

Near the end of the trip, the truck stopped suddenly. Three young paramilitaries with pistols under their shirts ordered everyone to get out, show their IDs, and have their bags searched. Everyone complied silently, eager to get back on the truck as soon as possible. The armed men began searching the truck.

Scott suggested that we stay and observe the activities at this checkpoint. I agreed and began writing conspicuously in my notebook, while Scott pulled out a very threatening weapon: a disposable camera. The young paramilitaries covered their faces with bandanas while their leader demanded the camera. Scott apologized, but explained that it was necessary for us to document human-rights violations and that we would not use the photos to endanger the three of them.

When the search was finished, the people boarded the truck again. One of the *campesinos* boarding the truck said quietly, "We have no choice. We have to do what they say." He seemed to wish that he could join us in resistance.

Scott and I decided we would stay at the checkpoint. This stunned the paramilitaries, who resumed searching any other vehicles that came by. We tried to talk to the men as we continued taking photos. We told them why we were there, that we were working for peace in Colombia. We prayed and sang "Nada te turbe" ("Let nothing distress you"). Their fear was evident; they knew that any wrong move could lead to death at the hands of their superiors.

Who are the paramilitaries? They can be thirty-something commanders, they can be teenagers, or they can be young men in their early twenties. Guerrillas can be even younger. The guerrilla groups admittedly recruit kids aged fifteen and older, and they accept much younger children. A guerrilla commander once bragged to Scott and me that he had a nine-year-old boy in his ranks. "Do you want to see him?" he asked us eagerly. "No," said Scott, disgusted. We were there to talk about peace and respect for civilians in a conflict that had left millions displaced from their homes. We were not there to watch an unrepentant killer gleefully flaunt international law. The commander seemed to fear no one, but what was his bravado hiding? What pain did he hold inside that could only be dulled by large quantities of beer or *aguardiente* liquor?

The paramilitaries openly controlled the city where we lived and were more visible to us than the guerrillas. They also traveled in broad daylight, without fear of police or the army. Their collusion with Colombian government forces was so well known that it was accepted as a fact of life. The army used the paramilitary to carry out its dirty work and avoid responsibility for civilian deaths. It was so taken for granted that the paramilitary commander patiently explained to me and Scott, "We are here in collaboration with the police and army." He was responding to our demands to know why the paramilitaries were extorting money from all passersby.

As Scott and I stood facing the three armed paramilitaries who had stopped us on the road, exhilaration overcame any sense of danger. Scott's confidence in our mission and my perception of the young men's fear convinced me they would not hurt us. Fear and doubt had been overcome as we emerged from the interaction feeling victorious. Surely, once David had conquered Goliath he had no more fear. But after all his celebrations were over, did he go see his therapist and confess that he had actually been afraid of Goliath at first?

Though I ignored it, my fear did not go away. Rather, it emerged months later as headaches, depression, fatigue, nightmares, and anxiety, even though I continued to claim that I had not felt in personal danger at any point.

I had believed that by joining CPT, I would fear nothing. Through the prayer and worship of our committed team, I'd be protected by God's light, and fear would be cast out. I imagined that a month of training in nonviolence would magically transform me into one of the courageous CPTers I so admired.

But once I arrived in Colombia, I was constantly anxious about doing the wrong thing, saying the wrong words, misunderstanding the heavily accented Spanish in the countryside, or committing some other cultural faux pas. I wouldn't admit any of this to my teammates, because I wanted to be trusted as a strong team member. And I certainly wouldn't admit that I had

A Colombian civilian is stopped at a road-side checkpoint.

been afraid in a crisis situation, since that is when I most need to call on the skills we'd learned in training.

The Bible says again and again that we are not to be afraid, for God is with us. This led me to feel that it was unchristian to fear. In CPT training, we hadn't talked about being afraid, and I thought it was a lack of faith, a lack of love, that produced fear in me. I worked hard to shut it out and hoped it would go away.

Why was I afraid? For many reasons. To begin with, my own country did not want CPT working in Colombia. Americans are a target of the guerrillas, says the State Department. And in Barrancabermeja (Barranca), the paramilitary-controlled city where the CPT team is based, anyone working for peace is a target. Peacemakers are threatening to anyone whose income or political power comes from war making. Armed groups especially target those Colombians demanding that their communities be demilitarized. No one in Colombia is viewed as neutral by armed actors.

Once during our first few weeks in Colombia, I went for a walk with my husband, Charles, also a fulltime CPTer. We were eager to get to know the community and so explored some of the neighborhoods around the CPT house in Barranca. We walked a short distance along Primero de Mayo, the main artery toward downtown. The street was loud with restaurants and shops, and sidewalks seemed to disappear without warning. On the walk home, we turned onto a quiet street paralleling Primero de Mayo. Suddenly, a young man rode up to us on his motorcycle, with a boy of perhaps ten years on the seat behind him. He did not identify himself but demanded to see our IDs. What were we doing in this neighborhood, he wanted to know. Caught off guard, we stammered. We were just going for a walk and didn't have our IDs with us. It was the truth.

Though illegal, the behavior of this paramilitary, doubtless charged with patrolling the neighborhood, was considered normal. The paramilitaries had been controlling Barranca for more than a year at that time, issuing official orders, from the inane (all trash cans must be red) to the inconvenient (curfew at 9 P.M.). The worst of the rules were left unpublished: disabled persons, homosexuals, and other undesirables could be kidnapped, tortured, and killed. And the list was growing longer: human-rights workers, teachers, union organizers, and community leaders were all targets. Often they "disappeared," and families never learned what happened to them, because witnesses rarely spoke out against the paramilitaries.

The young man on the motorcycle ordered us to get home, and then sped off. But apparently we were not walking fast enough, because five minutes later he returned and wanted to know why we were still in the neighborhood. After the second encounter, we turned back toward the main street, shaken.

We had thought we were "off duty" and just taking a little stroll. But we were unprepared to challenge paramilitary power and had learned a vital lesson: for CPTers in a war zone, there is no "off duty."

Charles and I took a six-week break from late August to early October 2002. It was our first trip back to the United States in five months. During that time we visited family, spoke in churches, and attended a weeklong CPT retreat. We arrived back in Colombia, still a little weary from our travels, the day after our teammates Lisa Martens and Ben Horst had been detained by immigration authorities. Charles stayed an extra day in Bogotá to attend meetings. I arrived at the team's house in Barranca the morning after Lisa and Ben were released, and I immediately handled a near-constant flow of media calls.

Things had changed dramatically during the six weeks we were gone. The Ciénaga del Opón, one of the areas where CPT had provided accompaniment since the beginning of the Colombia project, had been taken over by the paramilitaries. They'd instituted forced labor and were operating openly in the region. The newspapers published a story that said Lisa and Ben had accompanied a guerrilla, the personal doctor to the regional guerrilla commander. In reality, they had accompanied a grieving widow and the body of her husband to the appropriate officials. But those in power can spin stories to their liking.

The whole incident was, for the government, final proof that CPTers should not be given visas. No one on the team had been granted a volunteer work visa in more than six months. We planned for the very real possibility of shutting down the project and abandoning those who depended on us to help them remain in their homes and sell their crops. If we left, warfare might force them to move to the city, adding to the poor families who reside in shacks on the edge of town, jobless and without prospects.

Fear lurked behind every corner. Which of our friends would be killed first? we wondered.

I began to despair and worry that the government would come unannounced to our door one day, search the CPT house, and take our files and other possessions. They'd already raided dozens of other offices of nongovernmental organizations in Colombia that month.

By November, I was continually depressed. The whole team lacked hope. Then in late November, on the tail of yet another cold, I began to experience severe headaches and fatigue, which began so suddenly I thought it was a virus or some strange tropical disease. I slept twelve hours a day, not recognizing the signs of depression in myself. But depression seemed part of this culture, which had experienced too much bloodshed in the past five hundred years, and especially in the past forty.

Eventually, I returned home and began learning about post-traumatic stress syndrome and other types of trauma disorders. I was tired but hopeful and had finally identified the debilitating illness that had plagued me for more than three months. Sitting at a desk in my parents' comfortable suburban house, I contemplated how I used to sleep peacefully when I first arrived in Colombia. Crowing roosters and barking dogs kept me from sleep more than the fear of armed men. What changed?

Once, when a teammate and I were setting up camp in Colombia, she had casually mentioned something that had happened just a few weeks earlier, while Charles and I were on break in the United States. A few CPTers were camped together, two in one tent and a third in another tent. Their bags of extra clothing and other camping gear were sitting in an open school building behind the tents. A group of either paramilitaries or guerrillas entered the area around 3 A.M. and began searching the bags. The CPTer, who was in the tent alone, felt helpless. She didn't call the other two, not wanting to draw attention to herself from the armed men.

A chill ran through me in the hot, sticky air as I heard the story. I did not sleep well that night, or for many nights to come.

One morning in early October 2002, we crossed the lake Ciénaga del Opón in the team's motorized canoe. I had not yet met the paramilitaries who'd invaded the territory two months before. I was nervous, but also curious to see them.

As my teammate Lena Siegers and I neared the shore, I saw the still surface of the lake beside us interrupted by gunfire. Our noisy motor drowned out even the sound of the weapons firing, but somehow I knew what it was. Armed men on the shore waved their arms energetically, perhaps to tell us to keep moving. I looked to Lena as she ordered our boat driver to pull up to the shore so we could stop and talk with the men.

Several thatched-roof huts of villagers we knew had been taken over by the paramilitaries. One room had been stockpiled with assault rifles, grenades, and ammunition. Olive-green military vests hung on a clothesline outside, and several young men dressed in camouflage were gathered on a front stoop, examining an assault rifle. Some were a little wary of us, while others responded to our greetings and tried out halting English phrases on us. They explained they were "testing" their weapons. The commander's lack of shame was sickening to us. He smiled warmly.

We were concerned about the families whose homes had been taken over, and about their children especially. What must it be like for them, living with guns in their midst? Lena asked the father of one of the families, quietly, whether things were okay. We knew him well and had accompanied him when he was under death threat. He smiled uneasily and said, Yes, things are fine.

We introduced ourselves to all the armed men, and they told us their names. I looked into their eyes and saw the nervous bravado. They joked, wanting to seem "cool" to their buddies. Most were in their late teens and early twenties.

We left quickly, unable to stomach more of the scene. I was still reeling that they would choose to "test" their guns so close to where we were approaching—fun for them, perhaps. Maybe they wanted to see how easily they could chase the gringos away with gunfire. As we pulled away from shore, my heart still beat quickly.

Back in the United States, my four- and seven-year-old nephews have recently become excited about ghost stories. They desire the heart-pounding thrill that comes from fear, and they request the stories before bedtime. But there's a fine line between a "safe" scary story and a nightmare-inducing one. It is easy to let fear rule us and take over our hearts.

I remember the ways in which we banished fear in Colombia. Riding up and down the river, greeting everyone we passed and often stopping to visit was a simple way of reminding people that they were not alone, that even gringos from far away care about what happens to them. Our attempts to water ski on a homemade board brought many smiles and laughter to the folks on shore, and part of the message was that peacemaking is an act of joy, in stark contrast to the deadly seriousness of war making. I carried a guitar with me when we went out visiting, and after dinner, when the night grew thick around our candle-light, we would sing songs of love, hope, and joy. Fear could be forgotten for a time.

The courage of the Colombian people also fed our hope. Their continued work for peace in the face of displacement or death continues to be an inspiration for me. I know that one day their work will bear fruit.

Fear is still present in my life, but I am learning to accept it so that I can choose to hope. I am finding that embracing my fears somehow liberates me from them. Jesus's words to his fearful disciples, "Why are you afraid? Have you still no faith?" remain a deep challenge as I struggle to be faithful to God. But I know I do not struggle alone.

CONTRIBUTORS

Matthew Bailey-Dick lives in Waterloo, Ontario, and works in the area of peace and justice evangelism within the Mennonite community. He has been a part-time CPTer since 1998 and has worked with CPT teams in Ontario, Chiapas, Iraq, and Esgenoôpetitj (New Brunswick).

Tricia Gates Brown lives on the Oregon Coast and is the author of *Free People: A Christian Response to Global Economics* (2004). She has served with CPT in Chiapas, Mexico, and Asubpeeschoseewagong (Grassy Narrows, Ontario).

Mark Frey grew up Mennonite in North Newton, Kansas. From 1993-1995, he worked in Boulder, Colo., directing a start-up Victim Offender Reconciliation Program. He joined CPT in 1997 and has served in Hebron and Chiapas.

Bob Holmes is a Catholic priest and teacher who has been active in social justice ministry with the Toronto Catholic Worker and as the Director of the Basilian Office for Social Justice Concerns. He has served with CPT in Canada, Israel, Chiapas, Vieques, Colombia and Iraq.

Joanne "Jake" Kaufman worked with CPT full time from 1996 to 2000, serving in Haiti, Washington, D.C., the West Bank, Lakota Country, and Mi'kmaq Country. She now writes and presents information about CPT assignments from her home in Colorado's San Luis Valley.

Wendy Lehman co-founded CPT's Hebron project in 1995, and has worked in Chiapas. She served on CPT's Campaign for

Secure Dwellings, a partnership between Palestinians and North Americans, and is now a grant writer in Chicago.

James Loney was a founding member of Zacchaeus House, a Catholic Worker community in Toronto, where he lived from 1990 to 2002. He served with CPT in Hebron, New Brunswick, and Iraq and is a contributor to *Catholic New Times*, a Toronto-based social justice newspaper.

William Payne was a full-time CPTer from December 1999 until May 2003 and has been part of CPT teams in Chiapas, Esgenoôpetitj (Canada), Barrancabermeja (Colombia), and Hebron. He is presently in Argentina working toward a master's degree in international relations.

Dianne Roe was a special education teacher after graduation from Keuka College in the Finger Lakes Region of New York until she left teaching in 1985 to devote her time to art work. She is now a full-time CPTer and spends most of her time on the Hebron project.

Matthew Schaaf grew up in Saskatchewan. He has lived as a student in Central America and taught music with indigenous youth in Guerrero, Mexico, and Winnipeg, Manitoba. He has worked with CPT since 1999 in Canada, Mexico, and Colombia.

Carol Foltz Spring went on a short-term delegation with CPT to Chiapas in 2001 and then joined CPT full time in 2002 with her husband, Charles. They spent a year working in Colombia and are now CPT reservists living in Washington, D.C.